One Hundred

ENGLISH

GARDENS

*The Best of the English Heritage
Parks and Gardens Register*

PATRICK TAYLOR

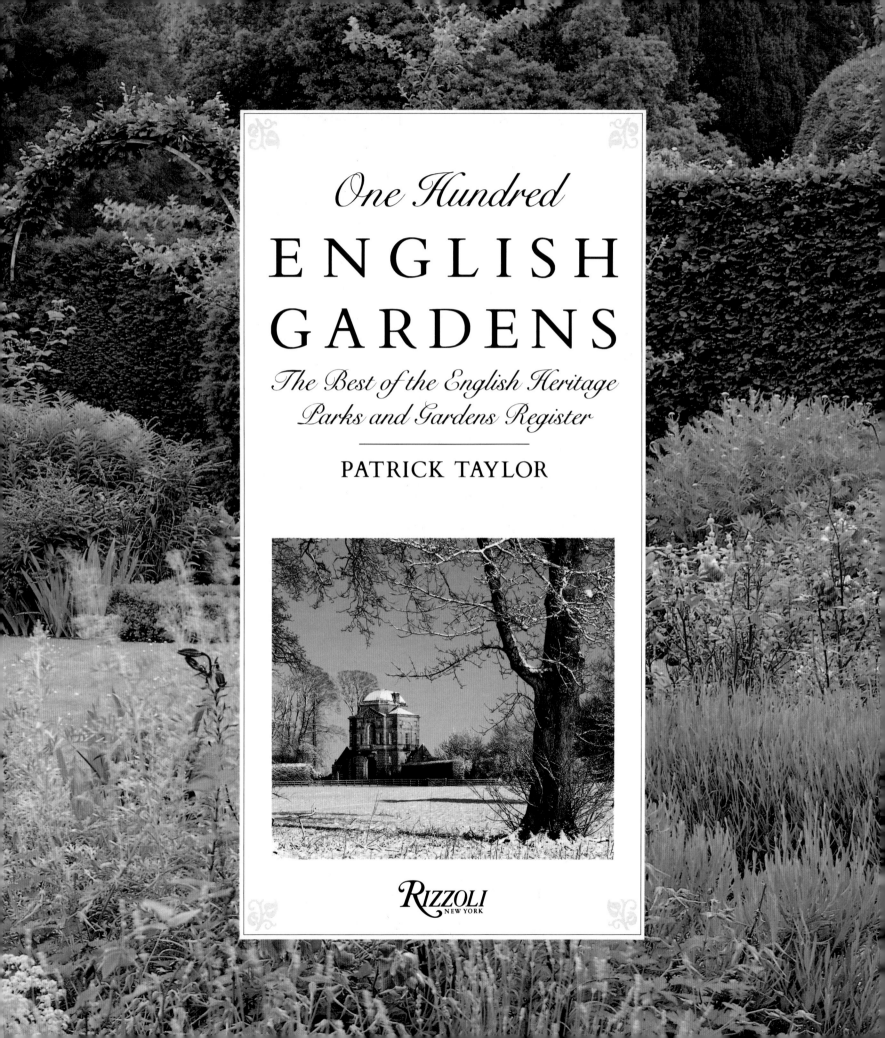

One Hundred

ENGLISH
GARDENS

*The Best of the English Heritage
Parks and Gardens Register*

PATRICK TAYLOR

RIZZOLI
NEW YORK

First published in the United States of America in 1996 by
RIZZOLI INTERNATIONAL PUBLICATIONS, INC.
300 Park Avenue South, New York, NY 10010

First published in Great Britain in 1995
by Headline Book Publishing

Library of Congress Cataloging-in-Publication Data

Taylor, Patrick.
    One hundred English gardens: the best of English Heritage parks
and gardens register/Patrick Taylor.
        p. cm.
    Includes index.
    ISBN 0-8478-1935-3 (HC)
    1. Gardens–England. 2. Gardens, English. 3. Parks–England.
4. English Heritage, I. English Heritage. II. Title.
SB466.G7T325 1996
712'.0942–dc20   95-31992
                                                                              CIP

Conceived and produced by Breslich & Foss
20 Wells Mews
London W1P 3FJ

Project editors: Catriona Woodburn
and Janet Ravenscroft
Text editor: Helen Huckle
Pictures editor: Paul Highnam
Design: Harry Green

PHOTOGRAPHY
Front cover: The Garden Picture Library/Brian Carter
Back cover, clockwise from upper left:
National Trust Photographic Library/Andrew Lawson;
English Heritage/Stephen Robson; English Heritage/Clay Perry;
English Heritage/Stephen Robson
Title pages: Clay Perry (2-3); Stephen Robson (3)

Color reproduction by Regent
Printed in Italy

Acknowledgements

Many people kindly gave me help in the writing of this book. I am in particular indebted to the following owners, or custodians, who gave me valuable information or allowed me to look at their gardens out of visiting hours:
Lady Ashcombe, Lord Feversham, Peter Frost-Pennington, Lord Gibson, Lord Ralph Kerr, Christopher Lloyd, Dr Malcolm Parker, the Earl of Sandwich, Lord Somerleyton, Victoria Wakefield and Rosamund Wallinger. The staff of English Heritage and of the National Trust have been very helpful, as have my publisher's editorial staff – Catriona Woodburn, Helen Huckle and Janet Ravenscroft.
I am deeply grateful to my wife Caroline for much editorial advice.

The publishers would like to thank the photographers of English Heritage whose work was specially commissioned for this book:
Christopher Gallagher: 34, 35, 52, 53, 60, 61, 70, 71, 86, 87, 94, 95, 116, 117, 120, 121, 132, 133, 164, 165, 188, 189, 198, 199, 210, 211;
Paul Highnam: 104, 105; Anne Hyde: 10, 11, 58, 59, 62, 63, 80, 81, 96, 97, 100, 101, 102, 103, 128, 129, 134, 135, 146, 147, 158, 159, 168, 169, 178, 179; Marianne Majerus: 22, 23, 26, 27, 30, 31, 32, 33, 39, 40, 41, 44, 45, 56, 57, 66, 67, 68, 72, 73, 84, 85, 88, 89, 176, 177, 192, 193, 196, 197; Clay Perry: 12, 13, 18, 19, 50, 51, 54, 55, 92, 93, 108, 109, 110, 111, 118, 119, 124, 125, 126, 130, 131, 136, 137, 148, 149, 150, 151, 154, 155, 156, 160, 161, 162, 163, 166, 167, 170, 171, 180, 181, 186, 187, 208; Stephen Robson: 14, 15, 20, 21, 36, 37, 38, 74, 75, 78, 79, 112,

113, 122, 123, 140, 141, 142, 143, 144, 145, 152, 153, 174, 175, 182, 183, 184, 200, 201, 204, 205, 206, 207.
The following agencies and individuals kindly supplied additional photographs: English Heritage Photographic Library (Paul Highnam) 209; (Kim Williams) 69. Garden Picture Library/Clive Boursnell 190-91. Lionel de Rothschild/Clive Boursnell 30-31. National Trust Photographic Library: (Oliver Benn) 114-15; (Neil Campbell-Sharp) 25, 48-9, 106-7, 194-5; (Vera Collingwood) 91; (Jerry Harpur) 64-5; (David Hunter) 82-3; (Andrew Lawson) 16-17, 202-3; (Nick Meers) 47, 138-9, 157, 172-3; (Marianne Majerus) 99; (Derry Moore) 28-9; Stephen Robson) 76-7; (Ian Shaw) 90; (Richard Surman) 127; (Robert Thrift) 43. S & O Mathews Photography: 185.

Contents

Introduction

*I*f the English countryside is a richly woven cloth, then parks and gardens are jewels and sequins to attract and delight the eye; the highlights and the focus to the underlying pattern of towns, villages, woodlands and fields. They are an integral part of that pattern, merging with it and forming an indivisible part of the whole. Something about England seems to engender a compulsion to garden, to lay hands on the landscape; every county has its gems, from Cornwall to Northumberland, Shropshire to Norfolk, each deserving to be recognised and cherished.

The tradition of gardening goes back to Paradise and the Garden of Eden. In England, it is not easy to find an unbroken continuity of gardens stretching quite so far back in time, but our gardens nevertheless have an impressive pedigree. Certainly the Romans were fully aware of the delights of gardening in England, as the excavation of the gardens of the Palace at Fishbourne shows beyond all doubt.

A shortage of records causes a gap in our knowledge of garden-making following the Romans, but once out of the Dark Ages and into medieval times, there is ample evidence that the urge to create gardens was alive and well. This desire has remained an unbroken thread since those times, a continuity of purpose which has resulted in the numerous wonderful parks and gardens which form such an important part of our cultural heritage today.

The builders of our medieval castles had a strong eye for design, setting off their creations by floating them in a ring of water, approached via sweeping drives over raised causeways. The great religious houses, too, were set within gardens and orchards, which, like the deer parks that accompanied them, abided by that fundamental rule of gardening – the combination of use with beauty.

Tudor palaces had their gardens, a series of walled enclosures with raised walks round bowling greens and formal water gardens beyond which lay the park and the chase. Then fashions in design started opening out, the close walled enclosures gradually giving way to grand geometrical concepts, straight rides radiating out across the agricultural landscape from broad terraces and wide parterres.

Next came the wiggle and the serpentine: paths began to snake and wind through pleasure grounds of evergreen and flowering shrubs. The formal terraces and enclosures disappeared, the ha-ha was dug to keep the deer and cattle in sight but at bay, and the lawn was brought up to the house. Drives from lodges in the enclosing park walls bordering the new turnpike roads were laid out across parkland. The park was strategically planted with clumps to break up the views across the old fishponds, now joined to form magnificent lakes, and out over the perimeter shelter belt.

The terraces were not gone for long. They were soon back, providing a platform for the greatly extended house, a balustraded foreground for the view, bedecked with bright coloured floral beds. The lawns of the pleasure grounds, set between the pinetum and arboretum, were studded with newly introduced exotics, and the kitchen garden became the focus of industry and new technology.

Gardening has by no means been restricted to the country. Most town houses had their gardens, high brick walls providing shelter, warmth and privacy. As the urban population grew, so too did the suburbs surrounding the towns. Here there was more room to expand, permitting the rise of the villa gardens where formal terraces give on to curving walks through flowering shrubs and specimen trees, to the paddock and pond – a country estate in miniature.

With the railways and the motor car came 'the smaller country house', within commuting distance from the town, convenient yet without the disadvantages of the ever-growing industry of the towns; cool green level lawns, gentle terraces, formal lily pools, herbaceous borders, peace and repose.

The pressures of overcrowding in the towns provided the catalyst for the creation of the municipal park, a splendour of fountains and bedding, pavilions and bowling greens, boating ponds and bandstands, civic pride and philanthropy. This combined with the quieter, pensive mood of the adjacent cemetery, planted with sombre evergreens echoing the spire over the gateway joining the Nonconformist with the Anglican chapel, watched over by angels.

Constrained perhaps first and foremost by the ground itself, the underlying topography, the aspect, and the type of soil, each fashion of garden-making has merged with the next, and each design has aged and matured with time. At each site, current trends have been overlain by the individual interests, tastes and eccentricities of the owners. It is this continuity and variety which make our garden history so rich.

It is an important part of English Heritage's mission to ensure that the best of our gardens and parks is protected for the interest, education, and enjoyment of present and future generations. That is why we have put together the *Register of Parks and Gardens of Special Historic Interest in England*, a list identifying sites of particular historic interest in the national context. It is of course necessary to be aware that gardens can be worthwhile for many reasons other than their historic interest – for nature conservation, for example, or their amenity value. There are currently around 1,200 sites on the *Register*, and the list is under review as more sites are added and as our knowledge of the subject continues to expand.

While the *Register* brings with it no controls such as exist for listed buildings or scheduled monuments, inclusion of a park or garden on the *Register* is a material planning consideration. This means that, if an application for development of a garden or park is made to the relevant local planning authority, the fact that it is on the *Register* as being of historic interest must be taken into account in determining that application. The latest guidance from central government on the built heritage gives welcome emphasis to the importance of parks and gardens as an integral part of the historic environment.

An enormous threat to the future of numerous parks and gardens is neglect. Many of the country's historic parks and gardens, in both public and private ownership, are suffering from the lack of resources needed for the repair and renewal of their basic fabric. This was highlighted by the damage wrought by the extreme gales in 1987. Just as English Heritage had put a grant aid scheme in place to tackle some of the devastation wrought in the south-eastern counties, a storm in the south-west in 1990 highlighted further the need and costs of replanting these beautiful landscapes. English Heritage is able to offer grant aid towards renewing the historic structure of those parks and gardens included on the *Register* as Grade I or II★ under a new grants scheme. The ornamental garden buildings found in many of our best gardens are architectural treasures of beauty in themselves, such as the 18th-century Shell Seat at Mount Edgcumbe, studded with shells and stones. We recognise that such features deserve special care and careful restoration and have provided help by buildings grants towards the repair of garden structures, and grants to Conservation Areas where these include historic parks and gardens. We have great hopes that both the National Heritage Memorial Fund and the Millennium Fund will allocate much needed Lottery funds to help save the nation's historic parks and gardens that are at risk.

English Heritage is itself responsible for a number of magnificent historic gardens: Osborne, Wrest Park, Audley End, Kirby Hall, Belsay, and Brodsworth, to name just some. For each of these sites we have a programme of continuous repair and restoration in hand, aimed at conserving and extending the life of the gardens for the benefit of our many members and visitors, now and in the years to come.

One of the most engrossing features of England's magnificent historic parks and gardens is its endless variety – variety in size, date, style, atmosphere, purpose. Every garden is different with a history and an interest of its own. Each is of value in its own right and as part of the whole resource, and each one of us who has a love of gardens and gardening is drawn more to some than to others. In the following pages, Patrick Taylor looks at the *Register of Parks and Gardens* and offers a personal selection of his own particular favourites. Supported by evocative photographs, he offers an irresistible lure to those not already acquainted with the delights of visiting and understanding historic gardens and parks, throws up suggestions for those already converted to the cause, and brings back memories, mingled with new facts, of those gardens which many of us already know and love.

I hope you will read, enjoy, and then resolve to discover more about England's priceless inheritance of historic parks and gardens.

JOCELYN STEVENS
Chairman, English Heritage

Helmingham Hall

The approach to Helmingham Hall is one of the loveliest in England. The drive winds across an ancient deer park, where red and fallow deer still graze, and the landscape is studded with oaks, many of which date back to the 13th and 14th centuries. The hall, which Sir Nikolaus Pevsner expressively describes as 'both grand and lovable', has the appearance of a remarkably unchanged early Tudor house – romantically moated, built of fine brick, and bristling with chimneys, gables and decorative finials. The Tollemache family who built it, starting in 1480, still lives here and it is chiefly to the present Lord and Lady Tollemache that we owe the exceptional gardens.

There are only traces of old gardens at Helmingham. South-east of the hall an avenue of oaks, planted in about 1700, leads from the entrance lodges across the deer park to the drawbridge of the hall. The park itself, of about 400 acres, is not mentioned as having deer before 1660. A famous old oak north-west of the hall was painted more than once by John Constable – 'A Dell in Helmingham Park' – in the early years of the 19th century. An aerial photograph taken in 1949 shows very little by way of a garden, although the splendid moated walled kitchen garden to the south-west is seen in full, productive activity. Until 1745, when the present walls were built, this island garden was protected from invading deer by a wooden palisade, and there is evidence that it is of very ancient origin, possibly even predating the building of the house. Today, the island, and an entirely newly planted herb and knot garden north-east of the hall, are the chief areas of ornamental planting.

At the entrance to the island an old parterre and its surrounding beds were restored in the 1960s. The box-edged compartments of the parterre are planted with *Santolina incarna* and in the beds that run along the walls there is an immense collection of Hybrid Musk roses planted by the mother of the present Lord Tollemache. Wrought-iron gates lead through to the old vegetable garden whose main axis runs through exuberant herbaceous borders. Cross paths are planted with runner beans, gourds or sweet peas forming decorative tunnels of vegetation. Behind these ornamental beds, fruit and vegetables are still grown, keeping the ancient eight-part division of beds.

The herb and knot garden was started in 1982 on a previously ungardened site. A raised terrace running along its west side gives views of box-edged knots filled with plants dating chiefly from before 1750. A grassy path leads between massed plantings of 'Rosa Mundi' (*Rosa gallica* 'Versicolor') beyond which are many old roses in lavender-edged borders. In the centre of the rose beds a figure of Flora, surrounded by golden thyme, narcissi and Madonna lilies, looks back towards the house.

The gardens at Helmingham, beautifully planted and kept up to perfectionist standards, make the best of their exceptional setting. Both ornamental gardens are arranged on an axis with the house, glimpses of which are constantly visible. This establishes a unity of house and garden that gives a marvellous sense of unforced repose.

LEFT *The central path of the moated former kitchen garden is flanked by impeccable herbaceous borders which are at their peak in late summer.*

OPPOSITE *The walled garden has been given over to ornamental planting in recent times. A pair of herbaceous borders extends away from the house towards a wrought-iron gate with the Tollemache crest of a winged horse crowning the piers.*

Wentworth Castle Gardens

SOUTH YORKSHIRE

LEFT *Broad Avenue runs up the hill to an obelisk erected in 1747 to commemorate Lady Mary Wortley-Montagu. Since restoration began in 1978 the gardens have made a speciality of rhododendrons, in particular the species.*

Wentworth Castle, of palatial grandeur, arose as the result of the rivalry of two branches of the Wentworth family both of which were anxious to claim the abeyant title of Earl of Strafford. The other Wentworths lived nearby and made the equally resplendent Wentworth Woodhouse. The estate of Wentworth Castle was bought in 1708 from the Cutler family by Thomas Wentworth, Lord Raby. The house that already existed, then called Stainborough Hall, was not remotely in keeping with Lord Raby's ambitions. In around 1709 work was started on a new east range, to the designs of Jean de Bodt, a Frenchman living in Germany. In the 1760s a south range was added in a style of chaste but imposing Palladianism by the architect Charles Ross.

As the house extended, vast gardens were being made appropriate to the scale of the architecture. Kip's engraving of 1714 shows a forecourt of the same width as the east front,

at the centre of which is a stepped octagonal pool and beyond it a vast double avenue, corresponding exactly to the width of the house. To the south are formal parterres and to the west a pattern of walks in a wooded 'wilderness'. An engraving by Badeslade in 1739 shows new developments. Crowning the hill behind the house is Stainborough Castle, a remarkable Gothic folly. Also clearly visible are the converging avenues of Lady Lucy's Walk and Broad Avenue leading up the hill. In the 1750s, the 2nd Earl of Strafford removed the octagon and the double avenue and landscaped the area east of the house in the fashionable new naturalistic style. In the 19th century there was a flourishing conservatory, a vast kitchen garden and elaborate flower parterres north of the house. By the dawn of the 20th century Wentworth Castle was among the countless great estates vulnerable to the economic and social upheavals that were about to take place.

RIGHT *On one side of Lady Lucy's Walk an avenue of limes climbs the hill towards the obelisk. Although the planting here is quite recent the avenue follows the line of the 18th-century layout.*

In 1948 the estate was sold to Barnsley Council by the last surviving Wentworth, but it was not until 1978, when Wentworth Castle became home to Northern College which still occupies the house, that a team of gardeners was put in to take the garden in hand. Since then there has been an immense amount of new planting, particularly in the woodland on the slopes west of the house.

There is an excellent collection of rhododendrons, which includes the National Collection of species in the *Falconera* group, many different species of Himalayan poppy (*Meconopsis*), several magnolias and countless Asiatic primulas relishing the moist, acid soil. Underlying this profusion of plants, and an increasing informality of layout, is the pattern of the garden that existed 250 years ago. The site of the octagon pool is now a car park. Where the great parterres spread out south of the house a broad lawn clearly shows the levelled ground. The two avenues of Lady Lucy's Walk and Broad Avenue, now softened by later planting, still converge on the slopes west of the house, where Lady Mary Wortley-Montagu's obelisk (1747) pierces the sky at their meeting place. On the far side of the obelisk the land falls away beyond a ha-ha revealing delightful Elysian views of the rural landscape – a striking contrast to the view to the east towards the M1 motorway and the sprawling suburbs of Barnsley. At the end of a grassy terrace the Gothic folly of Stainborough Castle still stands, dilapidated but memorably splendid.

Bowood House

The park at Bowood provides a fine example of changing fashions in English garden design from the 18th century to the present day.

Once part of an ancient forest owned by Saxon kings, 'King's Bowewood Park' was preserved as a royal hunting ground until long after the Norman conquest. The first knowledge we have of any gardening here comes from a painting of the house c.1725, soon after it was built by Sir Orlando Bridgeman. It shows a walled forecourt to the south and, behind the house, an avenue passing over undulating ground, and a formal lake.

The estate was bought in 1754 by the 1st Earl of Shelburne, who enlarged the house and constructed the walled kitchen garden and part of the ha-ha. His widow commissioned Robert Adam to build the family mausoleum in 1761, and his son, later the 1st Marquess of Lansdowne, employed the Adam brothers to do further work on the house.

It was the 1st Earl of Shelburne who, in 1757, approached Capability Brown about laying out a park. He wrote to his son describing his encounter with Brown, clearly uncertain that his money had been well spent: 'What would you give to know the consequences of the visit of the famous Mr Brown and the fruit of 30 guineas which I gave him? He passed two days with me… and twenty times assured me that he does not know a finer place in England than Bowood Park.' It was only after the old Earl's death in 1761 that Brown started work. His plan, which survives at the house, is dated 1763. The chief part of his work was to make a narrow curving lake at the foot of the slopes to the east of the house. He also planted trees in quantity – 12,000 hawthorns, for example, which cost £30 – and created rides and walks. Brown's park survives today in wonderful condition and, walking down towards the lake from the house, the view is one of the most beautiful of any landscape park. On the far bank, half concealed among trees, is a

little Doric temple, apparently dating from the 18th century and moved from the pleasure grounds north of the house to its present position in 1864. Concealed in the woodland is a superlative multi-tiered cascade whose roar is heard from within the woods before it is visible. The Hon. Charles Hamilton (creator of Painshill, Surrey) appears to have helped with its design in the 1780s and it forms part of an extensive late 18th-century 'Picturesque' garden of rockwork, including caves and a grotto, laid out by Josiah Lane who also worked at Painshill and Stourhead.

The 1st Marquess was keenly interested in planting unusual trees. When J. C. Loudon saw the gardens in 1838, he wrote that 'many of the foreign trees planted by the first Marquess [had] attained a large size, particularly the cedars and tulip trees'. The first monkey puzzle (*Araucaria araucana*) was planted in 1828 – well before the species became widely available commercially in the late 1830s. A Ponderosa pine (*Pinus ponderosa*) was raised from the very first seeds to arrive in this country in 1827, gathered by David Douglas in Washington State. Pineta became common features of Victorian estates but this one was a pioneer.

Since the mid 19th century a rhododendron garden has been developed in the woods

OPPOSITE *The Doric temple on the east bank of the lake was moved to this striking position in 1864.*

LEFT *The cascade was built in about 1785 with advice from the Hon. Charles Hamilton, the creator of Painshill. To one side is a grotto designed by Josiah Lane.*

surrounding Adam's mausoleum, taking advantage of a seam of fertile greensand.

The 3rd Marquess commissioned the terraces which span the length of the great Adam Orangery, overlooking the park. The Upper Terrace was designed by Sir Robert Smirke, and the Lower Terrace, by George Kennedy, was completed in 1851. Still with a strong Victorian flavour, the terraces are now distinguished by large and curiously leaning Irish yews standing between beds of massed roses and herbaceous borders.

Bowood is a large estate, impeccably kept by the present Earl of Shelburne, which offers many pleasures for the garden visitor. But it is Brown's park – one of the most memorable of his surviving achievements – that takes the breath away.

Hidcote Manor

*V*ita Sackville-West thought of Hidcote as a cottage-garden raised to the ranks of aristocracy by some special genius and recognised it, probably before anyone else, as a distinctively new kind of garden. It was in fact a pioneer, possibly the most influential single garden made in England in the 20th century. The garden was conceived as a series of enclosures whose contrasts of mood – through an eclectic range of decorative styles – were an essential part of its nature. This mixture remains to this day a powerful source of inspiration to English gardeners.

Hidcote was made by Lawrence Johnston, an American of the Henry Jamesian kind whose family had a predilection for Europe. He was born in Paris in 1871, had a French tutor, became a Catholic and took a degree in history at Trinity College, Cambridge. He became a British subject in 1900 and fought in the Boer War as a trooper. In 1907 his mother bought for him an estate called Hidcote Bartrim in a remote corner of the Cotswolds. There was no garden to speak of, although it had some fine old trees, including a beautiful cedar of Lebanon and some magnificent old beeches. It did, however, have an elevated position and remarkable views over the vale of Evesham. At first Johnston's interests seem to have been agricultural but he made friends in the neighbourhood with several people with a passion for gardening and began, himself, to make a garden.

Nothing is known about the ideas that lay behind the garden. There are touches of the kind of formality with which he would have been familiar from French gardens, and the influences of the Arts and Crafts garden designers are visible. But, unlike either of these traditions, there was a burning and very original interest in plants which, after trips to South Africa in 1927 and China in 1931, he introduced in profusion. As Vita Sackville-West wrote after her visit in 1947 'this place is a jungle of beauty; a jungle controlled by a single mind'.

Like Sissinghurst, Hidcote is a garden of compartments but it should be said immediately that the essential layout of her garden at Sissinghurst had been determined before Vita Sackville-West knew Hidcote. The compartments made by Johnston have strikingly different characters which provide a series of exhilarating surprises. At the garden entrance, for example, he preserved the superb clump of beeches (*Fagus sylvatica*) and gave them a setting that concentrated all attention on them. They are on a slight eminence which he treated like the stage of a theatre, making a vast lawn in front of them and enclosing the whole in hedges of yew. He also created a pair of dazzling red and purple borders, known as the red borders, which were designed to show their best in late summer and autumn, and in which foliage – both colour and shape – was as important as flowers. At the end of the two borders is a pair of elegant little summer-houses. Leading from the southernmost house, in total contrast to the exuberance of the borders, is a gigantic alley of hornbeam (*Carpinus betulus*) devoid of ornament but offering glimpses of the rural landscape beyond.

The various compartments that make up the garden, some quite austere and solemn, others overflowing with generous ornamental planting, provide a series of contrasting interludes. There is no overall predetermined grid – it resembles rather some delicious meal of many dishes in which the palate is repeatedly surprised and refreshed.

The rose borders in May with different kinds of lilac pressing in between columns of yew and the purple heads of the onion Allium aflatunense *soaring among the foliage of shrub roses.*

Bramham Park

The overwhelming importance and interest of Bramham Park is the survival of a splendid large-scale formal garden dating from before the period when the fashion for naturalistic landscaped parks swept all before it. The house, of cream-coloured sandstone and of a refined classicism, was built for Robert Benson, later Lord Bingley, before 1710. Although more than one architect has been mentioned as the possible author, it seems most probable that Benson himself designed it. Sir Nikolaus Pevsner wrote of Bramham: 'If ever house and gardens must be regarded as one ensemble, it is here. Bramham is a grand and unusual house, but its gardens are grander and even more unusual.' Benson had been on the Grand Tour in 1697 and would certainly have seen the work of André le Nôtre in France. John Wood the Elder, the great architect of Bath, worked here as a young man between 1724 and 1725 and it has been

suggested that he was involved in the garden layout. That, again, is conjecture and Benson himself is at least as likely a candidate as its designer. Wood certainly did a plan of the estate, published in 1731, which provides valuable information on its early appearance.

The garden is laid out in a grid of long alleys lined with beech hedges and animated, at junctions or at terminating points, by buildings or ornaments of very high quality. The starting point for this exhilarating pattern is the house itself across whose south-west terrace the main vista runs. Beginning at a summerhouse designed in 1760 by James Paine and later converted into a chapel, the main vista continues past a very grand ornamental pool towards a circular Ionic temple (possibly by James Paine) and culminates in a distant obelisk. The whole distance of this vista is about one mile.

Immediately in front of the house to its south-west is a modern formal rose garden on

the site of an old parterre and spreading out beyond it is the intricate pattern of beech alleys. The hedges here are very high, forming dramatic corridors of greenery. The visitor will cross another great vista, which runs past a formal pool and an open space with a Gothic temple whose design is taken from the Batty Langley pattern book *Gothic Architecture* (1742). The land has a gentle rise and fall, and at the south-western boundary is supported on walls at a higher level than the landscape beyond, giving splendid rural views. Although this is clearly a layout inspired by French baroque garden design it has a playfulness and irregularity that the French would not have enjoyed. Nor would they have allowed the glimpses of a rural world beyond, which to an English eye are so attractive.

Lord Bingley's descendants still live at Bramham Park and open it regularly to the public. The garden is beautifully maintained, and is almost untouched by the passage of time.

RIGHT *The Obelisk Ponds, built between 1700 and 1710, are part of an immense vista which ends at an obelisk one mile from the house.*

OPPOSITE *The meeting point of the beech alleys is marked by an early 18th-century stone vase.*

Hestercombe House

These gardens, designed by Gertrude Jekyll and Sir Edwin Lutyens working in collaboration just before World War I, may fairly be considered among the finest ever made in this country. It was a rare partnership in which Lutyens the architect was wholly in tune with Miss Jekyll the plantswoman. Miss Jekyll's planting schemes were not mere horticultural wallpaper, they became an essential part of the architecture of the garden, so that Lutyens' designs were strengthened by her planting.

'The Hestercombe gardens', wrote Lutyens' biographer Christopher Hussey, 'represent the peak of the collaboration with Miss Jekyll

The Dutch Garden has beautifully made copies of pots designed by Lutyens. The beds, edged with lambs' lugs (Stachys byzantina), have repeated plantings of catmint, lavender and santolina, enriched with roses and the creamy-white flowers of Yucca gloriosa.

and his first application of her genius to classical garden design on a grand scale.' The estate had been given as a wedding present by Viscount Portman to his grandson, the Hon. E. W. B. Portman, who commissioned Lutyens to lay out a new garden in 1903. The site was a marvellous one, with Elysian views

over pasture and park towards the Vale of Taunton and the Blackdown Hills. The house, unfortunately, had been rebuilt by Lord Portman, a clumsy Victorian mansion replacing a gentlemanly Queen Anne house. Lutyens therefore decided to plan the garden so that the house was almost invisible and all views were focused outwards towards the idyllic landscape. On slopes south of the house he laid out a broadly symmetrical arrangement with a square plat in the centre flanked by long raised terraces down the centre of which flowed narrow rills cut into stone paving. Running across the whole width of the garden at its southern boundary,

and linking pools at the ends of the rills, a pergola'ed walk allowed the visitor to admire views of both garden and countryside.

What makes Hestercombe exciting is the subtle linking of the different levels, the shifting viewpoints and, above all, the harmonious detail of planting and building materials. The principal stone used is 'Morte' slate. This local stone changes with the moods of the weather, from dull grey to lustrous green. Lutyens harmonised his construction by using the local 'drystone' style, which he incorporated into the boundary walls, paving, pillars and terraces. He then ornamented the garden with tawny

Lutyens' fastidious regard for local materials gives the stonework great variety. The steps are of blue lias, the walls of undressed Ham Hill stone and the balustrade of the same stone, this time beautifully cut.

'Ham' stone detailing, in niches, balustrading, carved masks and in the crowning glory, The Orangery.

Miss Jekyll's planting both emphasises and softens the architecture − for example, a pair of billowing myrtles (*Myrtus communis*) flanks one of Lutyens' grander doorways. It is also

constantly relevant to the site. For example, a well-drained sunny bed raised on a terraced walk above the plat is dominated by grey-leafed plants of Mediterranean character such as cistus, dwarf santolina, and rosemary.

Hestercombe was at its peak between the wars. In World War II it was occupied by the American Army and after the war the estate was severely neglected. It was acquired by Somerset County Council who, starting in 1973, meticulously restored the garden, drawing on contemporary records. This pioneering feat of restoration brought back to life one of the best, and most enjoyable, gardens of its period.

Borde Hill

*I*n some parts of England the particular nature of a site – its soil and climate – will have a powerful effect on the style of gardening in that area. In this part of Sussex the soil is either lime-free or positively acidic, the rainfall is relatively light and it enjoys more hours of sunshine than almost anywhere in the country. This has favoured the cultivation of calcifuge and tender shrubs, especially rhododendrons – of which Sussex has some excellent collections.

The house is an old one, dating from the late Elizabethan period with fine interiors of that time, but much of its outer appearance dates from the early 20th century when it was rebuilt by Colonel Stephenson Clarke who had bought the estate in 1892. Nothing is known of the early history of the garden and its interest today comes from the collection of plants built up since the arrival of Colonel Stephenson Clarke. He was one of those gentleman gardeners who helped to finance the plant-hunting expeditions which flourished at the turn of the century. Many of the trees and shrubs at Borde Hill were raised

from seed gathered in the wild and some date from the first introductions to Europe. The raising of plants from wild gathered seed has a real purpose, as seed gathered in the artificial context of gardens will often be fertilised by other species, diluting the true identity of the plant.

Although there are some good borders by the house, and a formal rose garden, the essential character is one of an informal woodland garden laid out to display the plants in a more or less naturalistic setting, with concentrations of different groups of plants in different areas. These, especially in the spring, will give pleasure to any visitor who enjoys distinguished flowering shrubs and fine trees. But there is an additional pleasure for lovers of rarities. Just behind the entrance lodge, for example, is in the words of its discoverer E. H. Wilson 'one of the most strikingly beautiful trees of Chinese forests' – *Emmenopterys henryi*. This particular specimen was planted in 1928, raised from seed gathered in south-west China by another great plant collector, George Forrest. To one side of the walled garden is a splendid old *Magnolia delavayi* – 'the finest of all evergreen flowering trees' in the words of W. J. Bean. Discovered by Père Delavay in Yunnan in 1886, it first flowered in the west at Kew in 1908 and this magnificent specimen at Borde Hill was planted as early as 1910.

Camellias have been a particular interest at Borde Hill and both 'Donation' and 'Salutation' were created here. There is an excellent collection of rhododendrons, including many of the rarely seen species as well the highly decorative cultivars such as the Knap Hill azaleas. Eucryphias, beautiful stuartias, a superb collection of hickories, many magnolias and countless other distinguished woody plants are found here. The gardens suffered grievously in the devastating storm of 1987 but it is an indication of the wealth of the garden that so much of real interest and beauty is still to be seen.

ABOVE *Penstemons fringe the Bride's Pool from which there are views southwards over wooded parkland.*

RIGHT *Chusan palms rise up behind a clump of the dahlia 'Bishop of Llandaff' in the Long Walk.*

Montacute House

'Here is a Somerset garden filled with the best spirit of its time, embodying all that is good in the character of the old garden world, and a valuable exemplar of the sunny glories of the ancient pleasaunce,' wrote *Country Life*, rather breathlessly, in 1898. Montacute, both house and garden, does indeed preserve much character from the past and is one of the loveliest ensembles in the country. When Pevsner wrote 'There are those for whom Montacute remains the most lovable of Elizabethan houses' he must surely have been including himself among them. The house was built at the very end of the 16th century for Sir Edward Phelips who trained as a lawyer, became a Member of Parliament and held lucrative Crown appointments. It is built in an E-plan with Dutch gables and a balustraded parapet bristling with finials – the whole made of golden Ham Hill stone – and a garden of terraces, balustrades and gazebos. It is described by Gerard in 1630 as having 'large and spacious Courtes, gardens, orchards, a parke'.

In 1787 a new entrance was made on the west front, liberating the exquisite east court, with its balustrades, elaborate finials and ogee-roofed gazebos for garden purposes. In 1845 when William Phelips married Ellen Helyar of nearby Coker Court his bride brought with her an excellent gardener, Mr Pridham. Under him the west drive was embellished with an avenue of Irish yews (*Taxus baccata* 'Fastigiata') and mixed cedars of Lebanon (*Cedrus libani libani*) and Wellingtonias (*Sequoiadendron giganteum*). The north garden was also replanted in Mr Pridham's time and the Elizabethan mount replaced by a central fountain and elaborate parterres. By 1898 when it was described for *Country Life* it had been drastically simplified, much to its present-day appearance – a balustraded pool at the centre of a sunken lawn surrounded by terraces with clipped Irish yews.

A watercolour by G. S. Elgood of 1886 shows borders against the south-facing wall of the east forecourt. The planting is chiefly herbaceous, with sunflowers and scarlet zinnias. These borders were subsequently replanted in the 1950s both by Vita Sackville-West (who spent her honeymoon at Coker Court) – her arrangement was thought to be too pale in colour for the stone – and by Mrs Phyllis Reiss of another distinguished local house, Tintinhull House. She chose a bold, richly coloured scheme with repeated plantings of *Cotinus coggygria* 'Royal Purple', deep red penstemons, sages and clouds of white *Clematis recta* and *Thalictrum flavum glaucum*. Another successful 20th-century addition is the border of shrub roses underplanted with *Hosta fortunei* var. *hyacinthina* which lies on the north side of the terrace which separates the east forecourt from the sunken garden. This was laid out in the late 1940s by Vita Sackville-West and Graham Stuart Thomas and mixes such species roses as *R. glauca* and *R. moyesii* with old cultivars known to have been in cultivation when the house was built such as *R.* × *alba* 'Alba Maxima' and *R. gallica* var. *officinalis*.

The Phelips family lingered on at Montacute until the end of the 19th century by which time they were running out of money. The house was leased to Lord Curzon, who entertained his mistress Elinor Glyn there, and was then bought by the remarkable millionaire recluse Ernest Cook, of the same family as the Thomas Cook travel agency, whose hobby was rescuing historic houses. In 1931, long stripped of its original furnishings, it was presented to the National Trust.

In the east court, boldly coloured borders are enhanced by the background of golden-brown Ham Hill stone. Here the brilliant yellow of achilleas contrasts with the sombre purple foliage of berberis and cotinus.

Penns in the Rocks

Some gardens are inward looking, referring only to the house which they surround and their various ingredients. Others, of which Penns in the Rocks is a prime example, have a remarkable site which imposes itself on the form taken by the garden. Here, in the Weald, on the border of Sussex and Kent, there are still many hidden parts of the rural landscape, entirely unspoilt and often dramatically beautiful. On the edge of the ancient Ashdown Forest, Penns in the

estate was bought by Lady Dorothy Wellesley, whose husband became the 7th Duke of Wellington. Lady Dorothy was a poet and friend of poets, among whom was Vita Sackville-West with whom she shared a passion for gardening. This is, in fact, Sackville country; Vita Sackville-West is buried in the Sackville chapel in St Michael's Church nearby at Withyam. Lady Dorothy built a Temple of Friends on an eminence looking down towards the south front of the

Rocks has an elevated site commanding views of the undulating well-wooded country. Its name is derived from William Penn who lived here in the late 17th century. The 'rocks' still survive, an outcrop of Wealden sandstone, erupting from the ground immediately south of the house to make a striking contrast with the attractive Georgian (*c.* 1730) façade of the house on that side.

Almost nothing is known of the garden history before the 20th century. In 1928 the

house. Here she particularly commemorated 'the poets who loved Penns', among whom was W. B. Yeats. A grassy path leads up to the Temple through groves of sweetly scented *Rhododendron luteum*. Beyond the temple a glade of oaks is filled in spring with the Lent lily, *Narcissus pseudonarcissus*.

East of the house Lady Dorothy turned a walled former kitchen garden to ornamental uses. This in turn was transformed by the present owners, Lord and Lady Gibson, with the advice of Lanning Roper, into an

ABOVE *In the walled garden a central avenue of 'Conference' pears is ornamented with decorative interludes. Here, a pair of box-edged parterres are filled with lavender and santolina, with domes of clipped box rising at the centre.*

LEFT *The rocks, from which the estate takes its name, rise dramatically from the ground. Their powerful natural shapes make a brilliant contrast with the elegant façade of the house.*

intricate flower garden which intermingles crisp formality with lavish exuberance. An avenue of 'Conference' pears leads down the middle with three beds on either side, each containing three of the pear trees and underplanted with the rugosa rose 'Fru Dagmar Hastrup' which produces its pale pink single flowers throughout the summer. In the intervening spaces are two pairs of rectangular beds edged in box and filled with lavender and santolina, crowned with domed shapes of clipped box. The beds that run round the

walls are boldly planted and specimen trees are planted in the grass. Here is a beautiful *Styrax japonica* and more recent additions of *S. hemsleyana* and *S. obassia*. This combination of firm design, fastidious plantsmanship and richly planted borders is, perhaps, the distinctive English garden style of the second half of the 20th century. Although this enclosure is connected visually, by extended avenues, with the rest of the garden, it has very much the flavour of the *giardino segreto*.

The essence of Penns in the Rocks is

probably best understood with one's back to the south front of the house. On the right, past a superlative cedar of Lebanon (*Cedrus libani libani*) the land falls away dramatically, with exquisite views of ancient woodland and a distant temple on the far side of a lake. To the left, towards the walled garden, are signs of more exotic planting, with distinguished specimen trees. Straight ahead, however, is the piquant contrast of the primeval rocks and Lady Dorothy's airy Temple of Friendship.

Tatton Park

ew gardens are as varied and as interesting as Tatton Park. The Egerton family came to Tatton in the 16th century but the present classical mansion, designed by Samuel Wyatt, was started in about 1790 and completed by his nephew Lewis Wyatt from 1807 onwards. The Egertons remained here until 1958 when the estate passed to the National Trust.

The first known gardening activity here dates from 1737 when an avenue of beeches was planted, leading as straight as an arrow from Knutsford town to the mansion. A little later William Emes, most of whose work was on the borders of England and Wales, was asked to design a park in 1768. Very shortly afterwards, between 1791 and 1792, Humphry Repton prepared a 'Red Book' showing proposed improvements. One of Repton's chief concerns was the way in which a visitor approached a great house. In place of the avenue at Tatton – of which Repton strongly disapproved – he proposed the present curving entrance which, at a crucial point, presented an attractively framed view of the house on the far side of a lake, Tatton Mere. He wrote in the 'Red Book': 'It is particularly desirable that the house should be at first presented in a pleasing point of view and if it is possible it should be all shewn at once, and not displayed by degrees.'

In 1818 Lewis Wyatt designed a great orangery which is one of the very few left in the country still used for growing citrus fruit. It also houses decorative tropical and sub-tropical plants such as mimosa (*Acacia dealbata*), bougainvillea and the Brazilian glory bush *Tibouchina urvilleana*. In the 19th century it was connected to the house so that it formed a floriferous, and sweetly-scented, family drawing room. A further glasshouse of special interest, and open to the public, is the Fernery or Palm House built in the 1850s to the designs of Sir Joseph Paxton. It is planted

in a naturalistic fashion, with a winding path between rocks above which tender tree ferns, *Dicksonia antarctica*, rise towards the roof.

Paxton also designed a spectacular parterre for the Italian Garden immediately south of the mansion. This was beautifully restored in 1986, using old photographs as documentary sources, and seasonal bedding schemes – for spring, summer and autumn – are now followed. Such elaborate schemes were common in the late 19th century but are rarely seen today, because they are so labour intensive. At the centre of the Italian Garden a stone figure of Triton – brought back from Venice by Lord Egerton in 1920 – trumpets water through a conch shell.

South of the house on undulating land the gardens become progressively more informal. Trees and shrubs are grown in grass and a long straight walk pierces the woodland leading to William Cole's early 19th-century copy of the Choragic Monument to Lysicrates. To one side of this walk is an intricate pattern of lakes. Here, in a shady, secluded place is an enchanting Japanese Garden, made by Japanese gardeners after 1910 at the height of the craze for such things. Nearby on an island is a Shinto Temple imported from Japan.

Tatton Park is in one of the most populous parts of England. It is maintained – to a high standard – by Cheshire County Council and gives immense pleasure to a wide range of visitors. It combines all the attractions of a public park with real horticultural distinction.

The Japanese Garden in spring, showing the fresh new foliage of maples and brilliant colour of rhododendrons. It was built by Japanese gardeners at the height of the Japanese craze in 1910.

Exbury House

HAMPSHIRE

Rhododendrons are a vast genus of about 1000 species, the huge majority of which were found in south-west China. They vary enormously in character and size, from quite small shrubs to substantial trees, showing great variation in habit of growth, colour of flower and shape of foliage. They first made their way into English and, perhaps more to the point, Scottish, gardens in the early 19th century with such species as *R. arboreum* and *R. barbatum*. Towards the end of the 19th century and the beginning of the 20th the trickle of introductions became a torrent owing to the activities of such plant hunters as Père Delavay, Abbé David, George Forrest, E. H. Wilson and Frank Kingdon-Ward. It is a curiosity of nature that rhododendrons, largely from the Himalayas, found in the temperate, usually coastal parts of Britain an environment in which they would flourish more vigorously than anywhere else outside their native habitat. They had a great impact on garden style, stimulating in the 19th century a taste for woodland gardens which sought to create a kind of idealised natural setting.

The gardens at Exbury, created by Lionel de Rothschild from 1919 onwards, were made during the last phase of the great period of plant hunting. Between the wars Frank Kingdon-Ward in particular, of whom Lionel de Rothschild was a keen supporter, made many brilliant introductions.

Exbury provides a beautiful site for a woodland garden. To the west it runs along the banks of the Beaulieu River and to the south along the Solent. This is a mild part of England and, although rainfall is not high, the humidity that rhododendrons need is provided by the proximity of river and sea. The soil is acid, rich in ancient leaf mould, and the lie of the land is agreeably undulating. Lionel de Rothschild, who was then head of the family bank, set about making his garden with astounding energy and formidable resources. He recruited 150 men to prepare the ground by digging it two spits deep, adding peat as they went. This went on for 10 years and these men were additional to the full-time garden staff of 60 and a further 10 for the glasshouses. Rothschild had already started to experiment with breeding new rhododendrons at his parents' estate of Gunnersbury Park in London. It is this activity that made Exbury famous, producing a prodigious flow of new garden-worthy plants, winning medals at Royal Horticultural Society shows and earning First Class Certificates and Awards of Merit with bewildering regularity. In fact he was interested in many other woody plants, examples of which may be seen throughout the garden today, and embarked on an arboretum – which no longer exists – whose aim was to collect every tree hardy in the temperate world.

The gardens at Exbury are now in superb maturity. Lionel's son Edmund is in charge and he has followed the family tradition of breeding new plants and winning prizes. The thorough preparation of the ground has proved its worth and visitors may see an exceptional, and exceptionally attractive, woodland garden at its peak. Over 200 acres can be visited and they provide many hours of rare pleasure. Rhododendrons with their brilliant colours are probably at their best in such a large-scale naturalistic setting – glimpsed in the distance or veiled by morning mists, they have the true character of their wild ancestors.

RIGHT *An elegant little Japanese bridge spans a stream, and the foliage of a Japanese maple makes a sombre contrast to the rich colours of evergreen azaleas.*

OPPOSITE *In spring the colouring of the Azalea Bowl assumes extraordinary intensity – emphasised by dream-like reflections in the pool.*

30

Hever Castle

The splendid moated castle at Hever is really a fortified manor house with bold machicolated towers to one facade but behind it a more rural jumble of buildings about a courtyard. It dates chiefly from the 15th century when it was rebuilt by the Bullen, or Boleyn, family of which Henry VIII's wife Anne was a member. As far as the garden is concerned, there is no record before the estate was bought in 1903 by William Waldorf Astor, the American newspaper tycoon who became a naturalised British subject and, in 1916, the first Viscount Astor. He restored the castle with great tact –

In the Italian Garden a cross-axis links the Pompeiian Wall and the Pergola Garden with Roman statues facing each other at either end of a corridor of yew.

'Nowhere is Edwardian craftsmanship displayed with more extravagant panache, yet without damaging the medieval interior', as Sir Nikolaus Pevsner wrote. The garden, although probably the most grandiose layout of the Edwardian period, is an attractive mixture of flamboyance and sensitivity.

Apart from the winding river Eden to the north, this flat site has no particular beauties of position or prospect. The gardens were

constructed by Joseph Cheal and Son of Crawley in four hectic years between 1904 and 1908 during which as many as 1,000 men were employed. To one side of the moat a consciously 'period' garden was made with a yew hedge maze and much yew topiary clipped into animal shapes. But it is in the Italian Garden east of the castle that W. W. Astor's most ambitious vision took form. In the 1880s he had been American Minister in Rome where he had made a remarkable collection of Roman antiquities and Renaissance statuary, and the Italian Garden was conceived as a planned setting for it. This great

enclosure, walled in stone, is divided here and there by yew hedges but, running along the whole length of its south-facing wall, is the so-called Pompeiian Wall. This, divided by the occasional buttress or embrasure, displays marvellous Roman busts on columns, sarcophagi, figures of animals and other sculptures, with climbing plants trained on the walls behind and the occasional substantial flowering shrub. The south-facing position, and the protection of the walls, creates a privileged micro-climate of Mediterranean character, appropriate to the ornaments. This is emphasised by some of the planting – with grape

The Italian Garden was designed to provide a setting for William Waldorf Astor's collection of classical antiquities. The Pompeiian Wall faces south, giving a Mediterranean flavour, and is divided by buttresses to create compartments for different styles of planting.

vines (both *Vitis vinifera* and its highly ornamental purple-leafed cultivar *V. v* 'Purpurea') and tender plants such as indigofera and the Brazilian *Abutilon megapotamicum*. Similarly appropriate planting of an entirely different character is found on the opposite side of the Italian Garden where a series of shady grottoes is handsomely

planted with astilbes, ferns, hostas and other plants that relish moist shade.

At the far end of the Italian Garden a grandiose loggia is embellished with a sumptuous Bernini-esque fountain and cascade guarded by watery nymphs that recall the centrepiece of some Roman piazza. The loggia overlooks a great lake, created by W. W. Astor, and excavated by 800 workmen. Anne Boleyn's Walk, with excellent trees and shrubs replanted after the 1987 gales, runs along the south bank of the lake. The gardens at Hever are fastidiously maintained and offer pleasures of many kinds.

Broughton Castle

OXFORDSHIRE

The setting of Broughton Castle is one of the most beautiful in England – the ensemble of castle, gardens, church and parkland extending away beyond the moat is one that few visitors would quickly forget. The house is medieval, dating from the early years of the 14th century, although its exterior, built of the warm toffee-coloured stone of these parts, dates substantially from the 16th century. In the middle of the 15th century it passed by marriage to Sir William Fiennes, the 2nd Lord Saye and Sele, and has remained in that family ever since.

There is no record of what kind of garden existed here in early days, and the first detailed knowledge we have dates from the late 19th century. The Fiennes had fallen on hard times and in the 1890s the castle was let to Lord Algernon Gordon Lennox who spent much money on remaking the garden. A *Country Life* article in 1898 describes what he achieved under 'the all-pervading influence of dainty and cultivated taste'. Contemporary photographs show a fussy and generally rather incoherent garden with a rustic arbour, corkscrew topiary and an eccentric sundial whose gnomon or pointer is made of clipped yew. By far the most satisfactory of the garden features shown is 'My Lady's Garden' and its essential design survives today.

Since World War II the gardens have been transformed, preserving the best parts of what remained and introducing new planting of real distinction. In 1969 the garden designer Lanning Roper was called in to advise on the garden. In his report he wrote: 'Treat area simply and play up the beauty of the buildings, walls and landscape.' This excellent advice ran exactly counter to the principles that had dominated the garden in the 1890s.

Running 180 metres along a west-facing wall between the castle and the moat is a virtuoso mixed border in which herbaceous perennials are planted in emphatic groups. The border is divided into two dominating colour schemes with yellow and blue at the north end, and pink, mauve, white and silver at the south with the occasional note of blue making a link with the other end. The late Victorian 'My Lady's Garden', hard against the castle walls, retains its original pattern of box-edged beds in shapes of *fleurs de lys*, but a wrought-iron basket, planted with tender bedding plants, has replaced the fountain in the middle. A quotation from *The Rubáiyát* of Omar Khayyám survives on the base – 'I sometimes think that never blows so red/ The Rose as where some buried Caesar bled.'

The planting in the beds that line the surrounding walls has been greatly refined by a recent head gardener, Randall Anderson. There is a dominant colour scheme of pinks and mauves with roses such as 'Belle Amour' and 'Ballerina' rising above a profuse herbaceous planting of campanulas, foxgloves, *Lychnis coronaria*, penstemons, pinks and violas. In some gardens arrangements of this sort all too easily become merely a jolly jumble. Here, impeccable maintenance and thoughtful associations of plants make it outstandingly successful. The visitor will want to scrutinise the detail of these borders from close up but access is also given to the roof of the castle from which the pattern of beds may be savoured and the exquisite setting of the castle fully appreciated.

ABOVE *A detail of the planting of the borders in My Lady's Garden – a cloud of pink and white* Lychnis coronaria *'Oculata' intermingles with pink geraniums and the rich crimson flower heads of* Knautia macedonica.

RIGHT *My Lady's Garden seen, as was intended, from the roof of the castle. The box-edged beds in the form of fleur de lys are late Victorian but the planting is entirely modern.*

Forde Abbey

DORSET

$\mathcal{J}$n well-wooded rolling country on the Dorset and Somerset border, Forde preserves an unspoilt rural character. It was a Cistercian abbey, founded in 1141, and still possesses a splendid Norman chapter house (latterly the chapel) dating from the 12th century. Indeed, it has features of most architectural styles up to the late Georgian period. After the dissolution of the monasteries in the 16th century the estate changed hands several times, passing to the Roper family, the present owners, at the end of the 19th century.

Nothing is known of the monastic gardens here and the earliest detailed information about the garden dates from 1727 when Edward Prideaux, whose family had bought the abbey in the mid 17th century, made drawings of the estate. These show a formal arrangement to the south on either side of the house – a layout which in essence survives to this day. For example, the entrance drive to the abbey, with its avenue of limes, is part of a long axis which cuts across the south side of the abbey and continues on the terrace beyond; south-west of the abbey a pattern of pools has subsequently been shaped to fit in with a formal scheme; aligned with the centre of the abbey to the south an avenue of black walnuts (*Juglans nigra*) and limes (*Tilia* × *europaea*), replanted in 1937/38, follows the line of a much older avenue.

ABOVE *Sweet peas first came to England from the south of Italy at the end of the 17th century. In the 19th century there developed a craze for new cultivars, all bred from the wild* Lathyrus odoratus, *and the tradition of growing them is still maintained in many country-house gardens.*

RIGHT *The south front of the abbey is shown from the far side of the long pond. The beguiling mixture of architectural styles – from the 14th to the 18th centuries – and lavish mixed borders with yew topiary are typical of the English garden. Traces of an ancient layout underlie modern planting.*

Despite the underlying ancient 'bones' of the garden, almost all the planting that may be seen today dates from no earlier than the 19th century. A striking feature of the garden is the easy transition from formality to informality in its various parts – this is no firmly divided garden of compartments. Immediately south-west of the abbey, running along a canal-like pool, a broad walk of mown grass is flanked by borders linked by rows of columns of clipped yews on either side. On the house side of the path, facing south, are tender shrubs such as *Carpenteria californica* and the exotic *Feijoa sellowiana* from Brazil. At the far end of this long walk the path leads into woodland where a figure of Diana lurks in the shade. There is a pronounced Victorian flavour in the woodland planting, with Douglas firs (*Pseudotsuga menziesii*), redwoods (*Sequoia sempervirens*) and Monterey pines (*Pinus radiata*) – all of which were introduced to England in the 19th century and quickly became fashionable. Here, too, is an excellent collection of ornamental shrubs and smaller trees, with good examples of maples, *Eucryphia × nymansensis* 'Nymansay', magnolias and pieris. To one side of the final pool, 'The Great Pond', a bog garden has many Asiatic primulas in the spring followed by moisture-loving herbaceous plants with striking foliage such as skunk cabbage (*Lysichiton americanus*), *Gunnera mannicata* and the royal fern, *Osmunda regalis*.

The gardens at Forde Abbey derive their variety from the range of different sites – woodland, water's edge and protected borders in full sun. The collection of plants built up over the years has the chief purpose not of astounding botanists but of providing a beautiful and harmonious setting for the exquisite buildings of the abbey.

The woodland garden is rich in native English broadleafed trees — ash, beech, oak and, here, hornbeam (Carpinus betulus). *In the 19th century new conifers were introduced from the north-west coast of America.*

Hampton Court

Hampton Court has always been a showplace. It was built to proclaim the prestige of Cardinal Wolsey and when King Henry VIII took possession of it in 1525 it was described as 'more like unto a paradise than any earthly habitation'. The Moravian traveller Baron Waldstein saw it in its Tudor heyday and wrote in his diary that it 'is considered to be the most splendid of the palaces' and described an elaborate garden with 'a large number of growing plants shaped into animals, in fact they even had

sirens, centaurs, sphinxes, and other fabulous poetic creatures portrayed here in topiary work'. The gardens in the 16th century were on quite a modest scale, lying between the palace and the river. The present day sunken garden – called the Pond Garden – is on their site, but the planting and the whole atmosphere of that garden is distinctly 20th century.

In the second half of the 17th century there were major developments in the garden. In 1662 John Evelyn described in his diary the

Bold foliage of Canna indica *'Purpurea' in the Great Fountain Garden.*

newly planted lime avenues and central canal put in place by the restored King Charles II on the east side of the palace – 'formerly a naked piece of ground, now planted with sweet rows of lime trees, and the canal water now near perfected'. This introduced a baroque scheme such as the king would have studied in France at first hand during his exile. From 1689, under William and Mary,

39

Sir Christopher Wren made his grandiose additions to the palace and an equally ambitious garden was made. The chief purpose of a palace and garden on this scale was to proclaim the importance and power of the monarch – in exactly the same way as Louis XIV had done at Versailles. Leonard Knyff's bird's-eye view painted in about 1702 shows the scale of the undertaking. Some of the fabric of Henry VIII's garden is still in place

but now four great parterres lie spread out to the south of Wren's new building. These *parterres de broderie* were probably designed by the Huguenot artist Daniel Marot whom William had brought from Holland. East of the palace is an immense semi-circle of parterres with many fountains from which Charles II's avenues radiate. To the north is an entirely new feature – a formal 'wilderness' of high hornbeam hedges with interstices

planted with elm – part of which still survives as a maze.

Queen Anne, who came to the throne in 1702, was intent on reducing the cost of maintenance at Hampton Court and the last reigning monarch to live there was George II who died in 1760. In 1838 Queen Victoria opened Hampton Court to the public and it took on the character of a public park which it has remained ever since. Today, much of

the layout of earlier periods is clearly visible, although the planting has changed over the centuries and the atmosphere is not that of the great royal garden of, say, William III. The Privy Garden, however, has been restored to its appearance in 1701/2. It is one of the most elaborate and impeccably researched pieces of garden restoration ever undertaken in England and visitors may see the parterres reinstated, bristling with statues

ABOVE *The view eastwards across the Great Fountain.*

OPPOSITE *In the Great Fountain Garden yews are shaped into flat cones and fine statues embellish the lawns.*

and topiary. The exquisite wrought-iron screens designed by another Huguenot, Jean Tijou, to run along the river front, were for many years obscured by a lugubrious shrubbery, but have reassumed their triumphant prominence. It is to be hoped that something of the original character be brought back to other parts of the garden, to enhance yet further one of the best surviving examples of baroque landscape in Great Britain.

41

Sizergh Castle

CUMBRIA

The Stricklands have lived at Sizergh since the 13th century. The castle, with its square 14th-century pele tower, was remodelled in the 16th and 17th centuries and now presents a finely picturesque appearance. The gardens, like the castle, have evolved over a long period and show a wide range of different influences. The estate is now owned by the National Trust.

The oldest part of the garden is the area of lawns and terraces south of the pele tower. The long wall dating from the 18th century that forms the northern boundary of this area faces south-east and gave protection to fruit trees trained on its surface. Such walls in northern gardens greatly extend the range of plants that may be grown and the fig 'Brown Turkey' still flourishes here. It also shelters the ornamental planting in the border that runs its whole length, some of which would scarcely thrive without its protection. Here, among much else, is the grey-leafed *Buddleja fallowiana* var. *alba*, the tree-mallow *Abutilon × suntense*, *Solanum crispum* and other relatively tender woody plants.

Leading south-west from the lawn is a gate, decorated with fine stone piers, followed by an avenue of the mountain ash *Sorbus aucuparia* 'Beissneri'. This elegant small tree grows rather upright, has very attractive copper-red bark and new growth, and makes an excellent tree for a small avenue within a garden. At the far end of the avenue a bench backed by a curved screen of yew makes an effective eye-catcher. Different kinds of ornamental planting enliven each side of the avenue. On one side there is a good collection of roses, either old shrub roses or, more interestingly, excellent species roses such as the giant Himalayan rambler *R. longicuspis* and *R. sericea omeiensis* which has startling translucent red thorns and distinguished single white flowers.

Steps link the rose garden with the so-called Dutch Garden, a term used since the 19th century for an elaborate formal pattern of beds with bedding schemes. Here the gently descending terraces of lawn had just such an arrangement in the 1920s but the beds have disappeared to be replaced by a series of pairs of domes of clipped variegated box marking the changing levels.

On the far side of the house is a remarkable rock garden which was made in 1926 for Lord Strickland. Rock gardens became very fashionable in the early 20th century, particularly under the influence of the plant hunter and climber Reginald Farrer whose book *My Rock-garden* (1911) was a bestseller. The Sizergh rock garden was designed and made by a local firm of nurserymen, T. R. Hayes of Ambleside. The rainfall in these parts is far too high for a true alpine garden and the rock garden is planted with a very large collection of conifers, particularly the dwarf kinds, many Japanese maples (cultivars of *Acer japonicum*) and an exceptional collection of ferns – well over 100 species and cultivars – which form part of the National Collection. All these thrive in the moist conditions and, incidentally, obey Reginald Farrer's first rule of gardening – choose plants that are suitable for your climate.

The rock garden is the largest owned by the National Trust and is undergoing a 10-year plan of clearing and re-planting which will further enhance the plant collection.

The rock garden, made in 1926,
is now fully mature,
with abundant plantings of
dwarf conifers, ferns and maples.

Port Lympne Gardens

KENT

There are few really distinguished houses and gardens in England that date entirely from the 20th century. This alone gives Port Lympne a particular interest. It was the creation, from 1911 onwards, of Sir Philip Sassoon, and it bears the emphatic stamp of a place made for a man of independent taste – there is nothing else like it in England. He found a fine position for his house on the crest of an escarpment looking southwards over the flat land of Romney Marsh with the English Channel beyond – on the clearest days the coast of France is visible. The red-brick house was designed on a virgin

The Chess Board Garden has squares of grass alternating with squares planted up with contrasting summer bedding plants.

site by Sir Herbert Baker who concocted a chastely decorative version of the Cape Dutch houses that he had known so well in his architectural career in South Africa. After World War II Philip Tilden added what the great garden designer Russell Page referred to as 'a cataract of gardens'. Page, who much later worked on the restoration of the gardens, was especially interested in Port Lympne: Tilden's design successfully broke

one of Page's cardinal rules – 'On a hill top site, I try to draw the main horizontal lines of a composition sideways. Paths or lines of trees plunging away down hill towards the horizon so often appear meaningless.'

Tilden's garden is a series of enclosed spaces, originally hedged in Monterey cypress (*Cupressus macrocarpa*) or yew, which spread down the steep slopes south of the curved front of the house. The Monterey cypress hedges proved insufficiently hardy and were later replaced with Leyland cypress (× *Cupressocyparis leylandii*) but the yew hedges, whose crests occasionally break out in

decorative curves or castellations, are now magnificently mature. Some of the enclosures originally laid out in geometric patterns have been impeccably restored since 1973 when the estate was bought by John Aspinall for use as a zoo. The Chess Board Garden has squares of grass alternating with squares planted up in red or white summer bedding plants. It is interesting to note that the planted squares are set deeper than the turf ones – so that the flowers are exactly the same level as the surrounding turf. The Striped Garden, on the other side of a formal pool, is a series of slender strips of lawn

The West Court Terrace is paved with squares of tiles set on their edges and slabs of stone. Clipped mounds of box in Versailles tubs are arranged symmetrically.

separating long beds planted in bedding schemes that may vary from year to year. Below the pool is a precipitous stone staircase descending to the woodland below – exactly the sort of vertiginous effect that worried Russell Page. The Leyland cypress hedges on either side soften its impact and the vertical descent is interrupted by cross vistas; below the two geometric gardens were a formal vineyard and a fig garden.

West of all this are a pair of mixed borders that sweep down the hill, with a central path of turf between them; these were completely replanted in 1974 under Russell Page's supervision. Beyond the borders a series of formal terraces are devoted to roses, dahlias and herbaceous perennials.

The visitor who stands by the house facing south is presented with the dazzling sight of crisply shaped and enticing enclosures descending the slopes. Despite the formality of the gardens they sit unexpectedly well in the landscape, with woodland pressing in about them and immense views beyond.

Blickling Hall

The approach to Blickling Hall is unforgettable – past a bend in the road the great Jacobean house is suddenly revealed at the far side of a long forecourt flanked by ancient yew hedges which are almost as old as the house. The house was built after 1616 for the Lord Chief Justice, Sir Henry Hobart, to the designs of Robert Lyminge who had also designed Hatfield House. Built of brick and stone it swarms with towers, gables, finials and elaborate chimney stacks – one of the most irresistibly decorative houses in England. The estate passed by inheritance eventually to the 11th Marquis of Lothian who presented it to the National Trust in 1940.

The external appearance of the house remains remarkably unchanged, and preserves much of its original character. The garden also, despite changes of planting, has been deeply influenced by the past. The enclosed garden to the east of the house seems to have started in 1616. It is shown on an estate map of 1729 with, beyond it, a central walk leading between two formal 'wildernesses'.

This basic layout was in place when, before 1738, a little temple was built to form an eye-catcher at the eastern extremity of the walk. It remains, in essence, to this day.

In the 1870s the Marchioness of Lothian, formerly Lady Constance Talbot, introduced an elaborate parterre immediately east of the house. The construction was supervised by Markham Nesfield with architectural work, including a new balustraded terrace, by Matthew Digby Wyatt. The Marchioness herself designed the new planting, insisting on the use of hardy plants instead of the bedding schemes of half-hardy or tender plants that were so often used. Illustrated in a *Country Life* article of 1898, the parterre shows a bewildering profusion of decorative devices. From a circular pool – embellished with a 17th-century fountain from Oxnead Hall nearby – spreads out an intricate pattern of shaped beds. Roses are trained as standards or up columns, and Irish yews are dotted about. By 20th-century standards it seems appallingly fussy and claustrophobic; *Country Life* refers to 'beds of simple character,

disposed for broad effect'. Beyond it there is indeed a simpler effect with blocks of yew clipped into the shapes resembling giant grand pianos, with pale stone urns standing out against their sombre colour.

The parterre was transformed in 1932 by Norah Lindsay who replaced the innumerable little beds with four square ones, each of whose corners is marked by yew topiary clipped into an acorn shape. Her planting scheme followed strict rules of colour: the two beds closest to the house have cool colours – white, blue, mauve and pale pink – while those further away are lively yellow and orange. Although some of the original planting has changed, these beds are maintained today in Mrs Lindsay's colour scheme. The disposition of plants is arranged with plants becoming progressively larger towards the centre of each bed, so that in later summer they form floriferous pyramids. The 'grand pianos' of yew have been left in position and now provide a satisfyingly monumental contrast to Norah Lindsay's decorative flower beds.

The Victorian parterre, simplified in the 20th century, is split by an axial vista leading the eye to an early 18th-century temple.

The Courts

The garden at The Courts seems to have sprung freshly conceived from the mind of its creator, borrowing here and there from certain garden styles, but clearly marked with a splendid independence of invention. It is very much an enclosed garden, in the middle of a village, inward looking and offering no views of the world outside. The house certainly sets a note of stylistic originality. It elicits from Pevsner's *Buildings of England* one of the very few emotional remarks in those unimpassioned volumes – '...wildly overdone in all its details, an instructive example of what a vulgar mind can do with promising elements'. It was built in about 1720 and has the appearance of something made by a local builder anxious to include almost every device shown in his pattern book. The façade swarms with a frenzy of pediments (wavy or straight), pillars, keystones, scrolled brackets and quoining. It was built by a cloth-weaver from Bradford-on-Avon who used the water, with which the garden is still plentifully supplied, for a cloth-mill. The history of the garden starts in 1900 when the house was bought by an architect Sir George Hastings who planted hedges of yew and box, dividing the garden in the architectural manner of the day. In 1921 it was bought by Major T. C. E. Goff who presented it to the National Trust in 1943. His wife, Lady Cecile Goff, planted all of the formal area of the garden and was responsible for much of the garden's character.

The entrance to the garden is unobtrusive, through a stone wall on the village street. A stone-flagged path, leading straight up to the front door of the house, is shaded by an alley of pleached lime; this is the broad-leafed lime (*Tilia platyphyllos*) whose large leaves flutter attractively in the lightest breeze. The chief parts of the garden are loosely formal in character but have little symmetry and are not related visually to the house. South-east of

the house, behind a yew hedge, is a curious arrangement of stone pillars which formerly had chains connecting them, on which cloth was hung to dry. Another relic of the cloth-weaving past is an irregular pond which had been used as a sump for waste flowing from the mill. A long rectangular lily pond was made by Lady Goff and is planted with mixed colours of lilies. There are excellent ornamental trees here which include *Acer griseum*, whose decoratively peeling bark is a lovely tawny brown and the Chinese *Koelreuteria paniculata* which in many ways is the most beautiful of all small ornamental trees. Its pinnate foliage when young is prettily flushed with pink and turns butter yellow in the autumn and the flowers in late summer are brilliant yellow panicles – hence its common name of golden rain tree.

South-west of the house, beyond a yew hedge which includes some bumpy topiary supposedly representing dancing bears, is the main lawn which has on one corner the remains of a tufa grotto. Beyond this is a formal border ornamented with a pair of tightly clipped silver-leafed pears (*Pyrus salicifolia*) and other silver-grey plants like artemisias and *Phlomis fruticosa*. This forms a distinguished accompaniment to the yellow and blue herbaceous plants that surround them.

A pair of beautiful Venetian wrought-iron gates leads through to an informal arboretum with cherries, maples and a cut-leafed beech (*Fagus sylvatica* 'Aspleniifolia'). On one side a hedge of holly has been clipped into 'cottage-loaf' shapes – another example of the whimsical formality of much of the garden.

The lily pond is splashed with water lilies, and richly coloured planting ornaments either side: pink phlox on the far side and in the foreground the scarlet Floribunda rose 'Frensham' rises among lavender.

Arley Hall

CHESHIRE

The present character of Arley Hall, both house and garden, was largely determined in the 1840s and 1850s by Rowland Egerton-Warburton – 'a good churchman, a good landlord, a good sportsman and a man of literary tastes', as he was described by a contemporary. The estate at Arley had been in his family since the 12th century and remains in the ownership of his descendants today. He rebuilt the house in early Victorian neo-Jacobean style and added a chapel by Anthony Salvin and G. E. Street.

Egerton-Warburton also inherited much from his great uncle, Sir Peter Warburton, Bt. The park had been created in the late 1780s to the designs of William Emes. Around 1790 Sir Peter and Lady Warburton laid out the Alcove Walk, a broad avenue flanked by walls and hedges protecting flower borders, which led up to a summerhouse. This walk, like another parallel east-west path through the walled gardens, was crossed by a wide north-south walk and all these ended in views over the parkland which today give the gardens their unusual spacious open feeling.

Rowland Egerton-Warburton further improved the design of the garden in the 1850s by making the Furlong Walk (named from its length) all along one side. This walk commands extensive views over the park and on clear days the Derbyshire hills can be seen in the distance. He also improved the Alcove Walk by completing the brick walls on the north side and embellishing them with pillars adorned with stone finials and a handsome pair of cast-iron gates. On the south side of the Alcove Walk he replaced the thorn hedge with stately yew and with a masterly touch added the topiary work and the buttresses to his own design in 1856. The borders here have been called the earliest herbaceous borders in England, but evidence of the early planting schemes, before about 1870, is lacking.

Originally there was a gravel path down the centre of the Herbaceous Border, but today it is of turf. Late Victorian paintings by G. S. Elgood show a much spottier planting scheme and a more hectic range of colours than is fashionable today. Since the 1960s Lady Ashbrook, Egerton-Warburton's great grand-daughter, has revitalised the planting with bolder groups, much variation of form and foliage and skilfully chosen colour harmonies. 'I believe', she wrote, 'that patches of colour emerging from a tapestry of varied greens and greys can be just as beautiful as a riotous medley of brilliance.'

Other styles of gardening are represented at Arley. Rowland Egerton-Warburton laid out a fashionable rock garden known as the Rootery which in recent times has been adapted to become the home of shade-loving plants and flowering shrubs. This may be compared with the Stumpery at Biddulph Grange created by Rowland's brother-in-law, James Bateman. The two often discussed gardening problems and Bateman expressed disapproval of Rowland's plan to line an avenue with the holm oaks (*Quercus ilex*) which today form a splendid procession of giant cylindrical drums.

Since the 1960s Lady Ashbrook, in addition to restoring the finest surviving parts of the garden, has added many new things including an excellent collection of shrub roses and a herb garden. Gertrude Jekyll wrote admiringly of Arley Hall in 1904 that it was 'the best kind of English garden of the formal type'. The formality has been attractively softened but the quality remains.

LEFT *A view towards the Victorian summerhouse that forms the focal point of the vista leading between the herbaceous borders. The planting is rich in cottage-garden favourites such as goat's rue (Galega officinalis) and scarlet Maltese cross (Lychnis chalcedonica). Spires of yellow verbascum and the plumes of Macleaya cordata give contrasting height.*

OPPOSITE *The exuberance of the old herbaceous borders is kept in check by the restrained architecture of gate piers and yew topiary. Lilac campanula and rich delphiniums are intermingled with the creamy-yellow frothy flowers of Thalictrum speciosissimum.*

Rousham Park

OXFORDSHIRE

William Kent, in the words of Horace Walpole, 'leap'd the fence and saw that all nature was a garden'. Kent, who designed the park at Rousham, was at the centre of a revolution in garden taste which saw the transition from a love of regimented formality in which, as Alexander Pope wrote, 'Grove nods at grove and every alley has a brother', to a taste for the irregularities of nature. The garden at Rousham, Kent's only unaltered scheme, is of special historical importance because Kent subtly adapted a slightly earlier, and much more formal, garden designed by Charles Bridgeman – so the change in taste is plainly visible.

The house at Rousham was built in the early 17th century for Sir Robert Dormer. In 1738 William Kent was called in to remodel both the house and its garden. Charles Bridgeman, a key figure who links the old formality with increasing naturalism, had made a new garden between 1715 and 1720. This was a mixture of bold vistas, geometric pools and winding paths but it is asymmetrical and at some distance from the house and thus not dominated by its architecture as an earlier formal garden would have been. Kent retained much of Bridgeman's layout – including The Long Walk which cuts straight as an arrow through the woodland. Bridgeman already understood the charms of drawing the

An early 18th-century lead figure of Mercury directs attention to Arcadian rural views beyond the river Cherwell.

outside landscape into the garden and was a pioneer in the use of the ha-ha, the invisible sunken fence that kept livestock out but allowed an unbroken view into the country-side. Kent, however, went further and positively focused the visitor's attention on what was outside the garden. He built a

lovely stone arcade, Praeneste, with elegant seats from which there are views of unspoilt rural scenes north-east over the curving river Cherwell. Praeneste is marked by a large urn at each end and glimpses of it are caught from many parts of the garden. Throughout the garden, all the statues except one are placed in a position to look outwards as though to direct the visitor's gaze away from the splendours of the private Elysium.

Where Bridgeman had crisply outlined square pools Kent made the Venus Vale, a long glade through the woods leading down to the banks of the river. He altered one of Bridgeman's square pools into a much softer octagon and introduced a series of rustic cascades for the water to descend to the river. The statue of Venus on a stone arch at the head of the Vale is guarded by hissing swans. To one side of the octagonal pool a winding walk leads through the woods accompanied by a little serpentine rill. Kent uses statues almost casually, so that they are suddenly re-vealed among trees, rather than flaunted as eye-catchers or focal points. Throughout the garden there is a sense of composed, painterly scenes which shift with the viewer's position, and the irregularity of the layout adds im-mensely to the variety of the views. Walpole called it 'the most engaging of Kent's works. It is Kentissimo'.

OPPOSITE The placing of statues in the 18th-century landscape garden was done with great subtlety. Here, a figure of Apollo terminates a vista.

Muncaster Castle

The castle has a marvellous position on a bight of land jutting westwards into the estuary of the river Esk. Its elevation, 30 metres above sea level, which elsewhere might be insignificant, gives it in this position superb views over Eskdale which that fastidious connoisseur of views, John

ABOVE *The slopes below the castle are abundantly planted with ornamental trees and shrubs. Rhododendrons and maples take on autumn colours, with exquisite views of Eskdale beyond.*

OPPOSITE *The castle framed by the foliage of old rhododendrons.*

Ruskin, described as 'the gateway to Paradise'. The castle, built of handsome pink granite, was started in 1325 on a site further from the sea than an earlier habitation – 'better and more conveniently set for state and avoidance of air, and sharp distempers from the sea' as a 17th-century account put it. The castle, however, owes its present appearance chiefly to Anthony Salvin who rebuilt it between 1860 and 1866. The Pennington family has been associated with Muncaster since the 13th century.

The deer park west of the castle was probably made in the 15th century and a 17th-century writer referred to it as 'a brave parke and all belongings to this grand house

of Moncastre full of fallow deer'. Not long after 1769, in the time of Sir Joseph Pennington, landscaping was carried out; part of the park was incorporated into the designed landscape and a belt of trees was planted to the east of the castle to give it the appearance, according to the fashion of the

time, of rising from the greenery. A little later, around 1780, a magnificent new feature, the Terrace, was added, to give prospects of the finest scenery. The Terrace was extended in 1860 and at this time a boundary hedge of box was planted with alternating pillars of green and golden yew. In the 1790s immense numbers of hardwood trees were added –

almost 50,000 between 1793 and 1794. In 1893 an article on the garden in the *Gardener's Chronicle* provides the first mention of what was to become a major theme at Muncaster – 'large numbers of all kinds of Rhododendrons and Azaleas . . . fine specimens of *Rhododendron jacksonii, R. praecox* and *R. hirsutum,* and many of the beautiful hybrids'. Recently discovered photographs, taken in 1860, show a planting of young rhododendrons along the edge of the Ghyll, a sharp deep valley. These hybrids are now 14 to 15 metres tall and are among the tallest in Britain. In the early 20th century this collection was given great stimulus by Sir John Ramsden who inherited the estate in 1917. Sir John subscribed to many of the plant-hunting expeditions between the wars, particularly those undertaken jointly by Frank Ludlow and George Sherriff from 1933 onwards, and those of George Forrest and of Frank Kingdon-Ward. A 1924 expedition through south-east Tibet by Kingdon-Ward and Sir John's cousin, Earl Cawdor, introduced many new species of rhododendron which still thrive at Muncaster, one named *R. ramsdenianum* in Sir John's honour. Streams of new plants, especially rhododendrons, made their way to Muncaster where the climate, with high rainfall and relatively mild winters, provided an exceptional environment for rhododendrons. Furthermore the richly planted slopes, rising to 90 metres behind the castle, gave excellent protection from the sometimes violent prevailing winds and a superb setting.

The gardens at Muncaster, like countless others, suffered from neglect after World War II. There is now an ambitious restoration scheme afoot, with plans to use only plants of known wild origin and to extend the season by using a wide range of Sino-Himalayan plants. Meanwhile there is still much to see and admire, and the Terrace survives, offering the visitor an exquisite promenade and the same unforgettable views that so enchanted Ruskin.

Kew Gardens

SURREY

The water-lily house was built in 1852 to the design of Richard Turner. Apart from water lilies, economic plants are grown including the exotic loofah (Luffa cylindrica).

'The Royal Botanic Gardens, Kew,' says the current guidebook, 'holds the largest and most diverse collection of living plants and the most comprehensive research collection of preserved plant material in the world.' Unlike many other botanical gardens Kew is also a beautiful landscape, with a fascinating history, and a place where the highest standards of practical horticulture may be seen displayed.

The gardens are 'royal' because of their origins in the 1720s when George II and Queen Caroline lived at Ormonde Lodge,

Richmond on the river near Kew. Their son Frederick, Prince of Wales, leased the neighbouring estate of Kew and his widow Augusta founded a botanic garden there in 1759. Her head gardener was a Scot, William Aiton, who had worked at the Chelsea Physic Garden under Philip Miller and after Princess Augusta's death in 1772 he took over the

running of the combined Kew estate under King George III. The architect Sir William Chambers laid out the garden for Princess Augusta and made some superb garden buildings which include the Orangery (1757), the Ruined Arch (1759) and the Pagoda (1761-62) – and several others which have, alas, been demolished. The plant collections were being built up throughout this period and by 1789 Aiton's catalogue *Hortus Kewensis* listed 5,500 different species in cultivation.

In 1771 Sir Joseph Banks was appointed scientific adviser to George III which appointment made him effectively head of Kew. Under him a series of plant-hunting expeditions were organised to South Africa, Australia, West Africa and China from all of which a flood of new plants came to Kew.

The first formally appointed Director of Kew, in 1841, was Sir William Hooker who transformed the gardens. Under him they were opened to the public, with 9,000 visitors in the first year; in the year of his death in 1865 there were 73,000 visitors. He was succeeded by his son, Joseph, who had already made pioneering plant expeditions, especially to the Himalayas. His book *Rhododendrons of the Sikkim-Himalaya* (1849-

51) was a key influence on 19th-century taste for rhododendrons. The Hookers established Kew as one of the foremost botanical institutions in the world. Under them were built the Palm House (1848) and the Temperate House (1860-68) which are among the finest glasshouses ever built.

In the 20th century the scientific work of Kew has continued vigorously. Conservation has become a major activity and there is a programme of propagating threatened plants

The Palm House, completed in 1848 to the designs of Decimus Burton and Richard Turner, remains one of the greatest glasshouses ever built.

and returning them to the wild. There is great interest in the potential of plants as a source of medicines and a large proportion of all prescribed drugs now has some basis in plant material. But for many visitors the scientific work of Kew is of passing interest. For them the beautiful setting by the Thames and the immense variety of garden plants grown to perfectionist standards – including many superb old trees – provide the essential attractions. They will also appreciate the new Evolution House, opened 1995, which enables the visitor to walk through 3,500 million years of plant evolution – from primeval to the first flowering plants.

Abbots Ripton Hall

Almost entirely made since World War II, the garden at Abbots Ripton Hall has assumed a splendid air of maturity. The hall itself was built in the 18th century on the site of medieval abbey buildings. The grounds are flat, but well wooded and supplied with plentiful water from Abbots Ripton brook which flows through them. In addition to the hundreds of elm trees to be found in the garden and village (the result of 17 years of tree surgery and injection undertaken by Lord De Ramsey and his daughter), old woodland of oak, ash, maple and hazel, and more recent 19th-century plantings of chestnut, lime and plane, protect the estate from the sharp winds that sweep this famously windy part of East Anglia.

Although they have had the help of some excellent designers, including Humphrey Waterfield and Lanning Roper, it was the owners themselves, Lord and Lady De Ramsey, who were the inspiring force behind the garden, providing the unifying spirit that links its varied ingredients into a successful blend of formality and informality, allowing varied settings for a very wide range of plants, some of them rare. Lord De Ramsey died in 1993. His eldest son and family now live in the hall and his wife has enthusiastically taken over the running of the garden.

The house is connected harmoniously to the garden with separate enclosures providing surprise, intimacy and sheltered sites for vulnerable plants. The vistas which link these spaces, and much of the admirable planting,

An Edwardian-style arbour is festooned with climbing roses and underplanted with irises, grey-leafed Stachys byzantina *and splashes of magenta* Lychnis coronaria.

are chiefly the work of Humphrey Waterfield, who died in 1971. Waterfield came from a family of distinguished artists and gardeners and made himself a remarkable garden at Hill Pasture, not far away at Broxted in Essex, surrounding a modern-movement house by Ernö Goldfinger. His work on the gardens at Abbots Ripton is commemorated by an urn which bears the inscription

'Remember Humphrey Waterfield who made this garden anew. Nov. 1971'.

It is the strong pattern of vistas, and logical interconnections of features, that gives the garden its unity. On the south-west side of the house one such vista, visible from the other side of a canal spanned by an elaborate Chinoiserie fretwork bridge, is framed by an opening in giant yew hedges. Beyond the yew hedges, a wide turf path leads between a pair of deep mixed borders which are backed by pillars of Irish yew alternating with clumps of golden philadelphus. Here are roses (including the Hybrid Musk 'Penelope'), a rich variety of herbaceous plants, and annuals which are used to enliven the scene in later summer. The vista is interrupted by an enchanting trelliswork rondel, with uprights crowned with soaring Gothic finials, designed by the architect Peter Foster. Beyond it the axis continues between further borders, backed by yew hedges, and culminates in wrought-iron gates. But even beyond these the view is extended by an avenue of chestnuts proceeding into the parkland beyond.

One of Waterfield's innovations was an immense silver and grey border running along the red-brick boundary wall of the garden. Here artemisias, buddlejas, elaeagnus, eucalyptus and sage have a distinctly Mediterranean note, recalling the garden at Menton which Waterfield revitalised.

Abbots Ripton epitomises the happy mixture of architectural embellishments, firm design and lively plantsmanship characteristic of 20th-century English gardening.

OPPOSITE *Contrasts of formality and naturalism are essential to the character of the garden. An urn rises out of unshorn grass and everywhere a rich backdrop of mature trees provides a dramatic change of scale from the intimate formal planting of beds and walks. Ornamental trees within the garden – on the left is a whitebeam (*Sorbus aria *'Lutescens') – make a visual connection with the encroaching woodland.*

Hawkstone Park

*A narrow path runs along the bottom of the cleft, a
rocky ravine fringed with moss and maiden spleenwort.*

In a famous passage, Horace Walpole
described the ingredients of the later
18th-century concept of the sublime as
'precipices, mountains, torrents, wolves,
rumblings, Salvator Rosa!'. This encapsulated
the feelings that were supposed to be aroused
by the picturesque garden which was a wild
and dishevelled reaction to the suave
harmonies of Capability Brown's shorn turf,
placid waters and comfortingly rounded
clumps of trees. Richard Payne Knight, who
lived at Downton Castle not far from
Hawkstone, was the great theoretician of the
picturesque in landscape gardening. In *The
Landscape, A Didactic Poem* (1794) he attacked
the 'dull, vapid, smooth, and tranquil scene'

of landscapers of Brown's persuasion – those
geniuses 'of the bare and bald'. 'Bless'd too is
he', he wrote, 'who, 'midst his tufted trees,/
Some ruin'd castle's lofty towers sees;/ Im-
bosom'd high upon the mountain's brow,/
Or nodding o'er the stream that glides
below.'

Hawkstone was the ancient estate of the
Hill family whose 13th-century castle was
destroyed by Cromwell. In the second part of
the 18th century two generations of Hills, Sir
Rowland and Sir Richard, created a sublime
landscape which precisely reflects the ideas of
Walpole and Payne Knight. They were
helped by a superlative site, a dramatic valley
with cliffs and craggy outcrops of red sand-

stone fringed with trees. A circuit walk was made taking the visitor on a winding and occasionally vertiginous tour of the park. The walk is calculated to display the scenery, natural and man-made, in all its variety, with subtly arranged contrasts and surprises. At the start of the walk, following a narrow path hugging the contours of the hillside, the visitor comes to a stately stone urn on a plinth commemorating the Hill family's staunch royalism in the Civil War. Immediately below it a dizzying wooded ravine drops away at one's feet. On a hill, half concealed by tufted trees, is the White Tower, a brick Gothic gazebo with tracery windows and an exquisite interior with duck-egg blue walls and a cast-iron fireplace in the Gothic taste. Further along the walk the Monument (1785) rises high amid a grove of monkey puzzles. A spiral staircase leads up to the very summit where the visitor may join a giant statue of the Tudor Sir Rowland Hill, first Protestant Lord Mayor of London in 1550, gazing out over, it is said, fifteen counties of England and Wales. On a stormy day the howling of the wind will add the authentic sound effect to the 'sublime' experience.

In the distance, on the far side of the valley, the Grotto Hill makes a dramatic ornament against the sky. Here is an extraordinary labyrinthine grotto which was, as a 1787 survey of the park records, 'curiously ornamented with spar petrifaction's, stained and painted glass and other suitable appendages, and at the west end is a door opening to a gallery in the rock so immediate on the precipice as to strike the visitor with terror on looking down'. The ornaments have gone but the experience of the terrifying precipice may be relished to this day.

From time to time the walk will plunge into subterranean passages from which the visitor suddenly emerges either in brilliant light (weather permitting) or, in one place, at the very bottom of a sheer rocky ravine whose walls are clothed in moss and maiden spleenwort. All this has been magnificently restored since 1990 and is a remarkable and thrilling realisation of the sublime.

The Grotto Hill is crowned with a romantic ruin and paths lead perilously about it with views over the 'awful precipice'.

Somerleyton Hall

SUFFOLK

Somerleyton Hall is an exceptionally good example of a characteristic early Victorian phenomenon – the old house transformed by new money and equipped with a garden in the latest fashion. There had been a house here since the 13th century but when the self-made builder-tycoon Sir Morton Peto bought the estate in 1843 the house was chiefly late Tudor in character. Peto commissioned a new house from the ornamental mason and sculptor John Thomas whose grandiose new mansion engulfed the older house, keeping only the foundations and one or two interior details. Financial difficulties forced Peto to sell the estate which was bought in 1863 by Sir Francis Crossley, member of a remarkable Halifax family that had made a fortune in carpet weaving. His son was made the 1st Baron Somerleyton whose grandson owns the estate today.

The most extraordinary garden feature at Somerleyton was the Winter Garden, an immense domed conservatory attached to the north side of the hall. It was built at the same time as the new house and was almost certainly also designed by John Thomas. The term winter garden was used for a very large conservatory in which an elaborate garden was laid out, using the immense range of tender plants that had been flowing into the country in the early years of the 19th century. In Morton Peto's sale catalogue it is described

The site of the demolished Winter Garden. In the background is the elegant surviving loggia – now part of the tea room.

as 'a magnificent structure, unsurpassed by anything of its kind in Europe. A crystal building in the Renaissance style with mosque dome'. It also had a large central pool and, according to *The Garden* (20 April, 1872), the iron columns supporting the roof were festooned with 'Passifloras, Kennedyas, Fuchsias, Tecomas, Lapagerias, Tacsonias, Mandevillas'. This great building was, alas, demolished in 1914 but part of it survives as a public tea room.

The gardens today retain a pronounced Victorian character. If the Winter Garden has all but disappeared, other glasshouses survive at Somerleyton in a splendid state of preservation. In about 1850 Sir Joseph Paxton designed two ranges of greenhouses with ridge and furrow roofs designed to maximise light. He, too, probably designed the elegant plant cases, recently restored, that run along the south wall of the kitchen garden.

The great designer of parterres, W. A. Nesfield, worked at Somerleyton where he may have laid out the formal gardens west of the sundial in about 1846 and was certainly responsible for the semicircular yew hedge maze east of the walled garden. Such mazes were a common feature of the historicist approach of many Victorian garden designers. Between the hall and the walled kitchen garden are many of the conifers that were so fashionable in the middle of the 19th century – Atlas cedars (*Cedrus atlantica*), Wellingtonias (*Sequoiadendron giganteum*) and western red cedars (*Thuja plicata*).

The garden at Somerleyton has a long tradition of opening to the public. As early as 1863, horse-drawn coaches used to bring visitors from Lowestoft on Thursday afternoons – early-closing day. This tradition of opening to the public is maintained today – indeed it is the kind of garden that looks at its best when thronged with people.

OPPOSITE *Broad herbaceous borders in the walled garden have a dramatic backdrop of characteristically Victorian trees, including monkey puzzles (*Araucaria araucana*) and Wellingtonias (*Sequoiadendron giganteum*).*

Stowe Landscape Gardens

BUCKINGHAMSHIRE

Throughout the 18th century Stowe was one of the most visited and most talked about of English gardens. Several of the finest garden designers of the day worked here – Charles Bridgeman, John Vanbrugh, William Kent and Capability Brown – and they contrived a vast and complicated landscape enriched by the greatest collection of garden buildings in the land. 'Such a profusion gives inexpressible richness' wrote Horace Walpole in 1753.

The house at Stowe is conceived on the same scale as the landscape. The Temple family, sheep farmers from the Midlands, bought the estate in the 16th century. General Sir Richard Temple, a Whig politician of power who became the 1st Viscount Cobham in 1714, rebuilt the house and started work on the gardens. Vanbrugh, Kent, Leoni, Adam and Soane worked through the 18th century to transform the 17th-century manor house into a palatial mansion.

Between 1714 and 1720 Charles Bridgeman laid out formal gardens south of the house dominated by a central axis that culminated in a giant octagonal pool, shown in detail in a print of 1720 that gives a bird's-eye view. Although this is essentially an old-fashioned formal arrangement, to the west of the axis winding woodland paths give a new informality that shows Bridgeman to be an important transitional figure between the two styles. William Kent came to Stowe in the late 1720s and was at first involved only in architectural matters. By the 1730s, however, he was laying out the garden in a radically new idiom. In a shallow valley east of Bridgeman's central axis he made the Elysian Fields. This survives today, a delightful sylvan Arcadia with a winding stream and pools, overlooked by a domed Temple of Ancient Virtue designed by Kent in about 1735. Kent's Temple of British Worthies nearby is a curved gallery of stone with niches containing statues of heroes congenial to patriotic Whiggish taste.

In the early 1740s Hawkwell Field, immediately to the east of Kent's Elysium, was developed as a *ferme ornée*, an ornamental farm, which originally had a hayfield in the middle and today preserves an agricultural flavour with sheep grazing under the walls of James Gibbs's Gothic temple. Gibbs also designed the lovely Palladian bridge spanning the river south of Hawkwell Field. The *ferme ornée* drew inspiration from Virgil's descriptions of an Arcadian rural life. Palladio, some of whose villas were working farms, would have relished this homage to him, appropriately sited in rich pastureland with cattle grazing.

Capability Brown was made head gardener at Stowe in 1741. He was only 25 and this was his first major appointment. By 1747 he had laid out the Grecian Valley, just to the north of Hawkwell Field, using already the characteristic Brownian ingredients of shorn turf and subtly undulating belts of trees.

Stowe was the first garden in England to which a guidebook was published, in 1744. By the early 19th century, landscape gardens had become unfashionable and remained so well into the 20th century; in 1918 Methuen's *Little Guide* to Buckinghamshire described Stowe as 'a melancholy relic of eighteenth century taste… filled with all sorts of pseudo-classical erections'. Today, with Stowe School occupying the mansion and the National Trust in charge of the grounds and their marvellous buildings and ornaments, it is probably in better shape than at any time since the 18th century. It is an exhilarating place to visit and few will disagree with Christopher Hussey's opinion that it is 'the outstanding monument of English landscape gardening'.

A lovely curved arcade of golden stone – the Temple of British Worthies – ornaments William Kent's Elysian Fields.

Penshurst Place

KENT

A 17th-century polyhedron sundial stands in the walled garden. Such dials, telling the time in different latitudes and often also incorporating a moon-dial, are found in gardens from early Tudor times until the late 17th century.

ew medieval manor houses can compare for beauty and interest with Penshurst Place. Though fortified with curtain walls in 1380, the house has always been predominantly in domestic occupation. Penshurst passed into the hands of the Sidney family in 1552 and has remained in their ownership ever since. The house, with its almost untouched 14th-century hall and its splendid Elizabethan and Jacobean additions is set in a vast walled garden which in its essential layout goes back to the 17th century.

Kip's engraving of Penshurst Place, made in the very first years of the 18th century and published in John Harris's *History of Kent* (1719), gives a vivid picture of the house and garden and its setting in parkland. Not only is the area of formal garden enclosed by walls

exactly the same as it is today, but the arrangement of paths, hedges and enclosures has scarcely changed. The medieval deer park to the north of the house still has a few scattered trees of great age – the Sidney Oak is thought to date from the late middle ages.

The walled garden is on a vast scale, covering an area of 10 acres, and was made at different periods between 1570 and 1666.

Double herbaceous borders make a firm central axis in the walled garden running up from one of the original entrances. Penshurst is in the heart of the Kentish orchards and here apple trees rise above the beds.

The walls are of fine brick although the house itself is of stone in a part of the country where, apart from churches, stone buildings are rare. In the 18th century the walled garden had become neglected and its present layout, so close to Kip's view, is the result of a comprehensive programme of restoration carried out by George Devey in the middle of the 19th century. This historicist approach to

In the Flag Garden the colours are picked out in lavender (Lavandula angustifolia 'Munstead') and red and white bedding roses. A spring bedding scheme uses tulips to create a similar effect.

garden design was typical of its time. Although the walls are unchanged it is not known exactly how much Devey had to put back in order to restore its 17th-century appearance. However, Penshurst was never landscaped and, thanks to the 18th-century neglect that was due to a lack of money, it is likely that the original layout had largely survived.

The planting in the walled garden is no earlier than the 19th century, and much of it dates from the postwar period. Some of this makes conscious, and attractive, reference to the Kentish orchards, with an ornamental collection of apples and a garden of Kentish cobs. John Evelyn wrote in his diary in 1652: 'We went to Penshurst, famous for its gardens

and excellent fruit.' The patchwork of compartments is disposed about two axes – one running north and south and aligned with a gate in the south wall and the other cutting across at right angles. These both give appetising vistas and harmoniously connect the various parts of the garden. Two eminent post-war designers have added attractive schemes: John Codrington laid out the Nut Garden and the Grey and White Garden and Lanning Roper designed a double border.

In no other English garden does a walled ornamental garden on the scale of Penshurst's survive. With a high standard of maintenance and much good modern planting the Sidney family has also made it exceptionally welcoming to visitors.

Audley End

ESSEX

'Without comparison . . . one of the stateliest palaces of the kingdom,' wrote John Evelyn when he visited Audley End in 1654, but, he added, 'the gardens are not in order.' It was built for Thomas Howard, 1st Earl of Suffolk, between 1603 and 1614 and by the time of Evelyn's visit it was one of the greatest palaces in England. An engraving by Henry Winstanley of about 1676 shows a vast range of buildings grouped about two courtyards with, to the south, 'the mount garden', a rather severe formal arrangement and, to the north, 'the celler garden (or Wilderness)', a thicket of densely planted trees. Evelyn visited a second time, in 1655, and described Audley End as 'a cheerful Gotic building, or rather *antico moderno*, but placed in an obscure bottome'. He did, however, note 'an avenue of limes' and a park.

In the first half of the 18th century two-thirds of the house were demolished, leaving only the truncated central court. In 1762 Sir John Griffin Griffin commissioned Capability Brown to lay out a landscape park. The position of the house in 'an obscure bottome', in fact hard by the banks of the river Cam, was turned to advantage by Brown. He removed the old park walls to the west of the house and made great sweeping lawns descending to the river whose banks were serpentised in picturesque fashion. At the same time as Brown's work the architect Robert Adam was commissioned to design buildings for the park. In 1763/4 Adam built a handsome three-arched bridge south-west of the house taking the Saffron Walden road over the river. This is seen in Edmund Garvey's oil painting of 1782 with the river meandering across the foreground and the house half-concealed in clumps of trees – a thoroughly Brownian effect. In 1772 Adam also built, at some distance from the house on the far side of the London road, a domed Temple of Victory to celebrate the end of the Seven Years' War in 1764.

Perhaps the most original garden feature at Audley End was the flower parterre laid out in 1830, with the advice of William Sawrey Gilpin, immediately to the east of the house. This early historicist design was an intricate pattern of beds, vaguely influenced by 17th-century French baroque designs, but planted with mixed herbaceous perennials and roses. It was kept up until World War II when shortage of labour made it impossible to maintain and it was abandoned. In 1985 an archaeological dig revealed the original pattern of beds, and the survival of some records of the 1830 planting scheme allowed a splendid recreation of the parterre which was completed in 1993. The roses and other shrubs are underplanted with a very wide range of herbaceous perennials – campanulas, dicentras, foxgloves, lilies, peonies, violas – and tender bedding plants are intermingled to fill out summer gaps. This flower parterre is best seen from the first-floor rooms that overlook it from which the visitor may have an experience comparable to that of a Jacobean guest admiring the more sober parterres found at Audley End almost 400 years ago.

In front of the east façade of the house the flowery parterre, designed with the help of W. S. Gilpin in 1830, has been painstakingly reinstated from old records.

Sudeley Castle

GLOUCESTERSHIRE

The Winchcombe valley is very sheltered and Sudeley Castle, although in an elevated position, is protected by wooded land rising much higher to the east and the north. There has been a house here since Saxon times but the present building dates from the time of Ralph Boteler; a descendant of the last Lord Sudeley, he inherited it in 1398. The castle was forfeited to the Crown in the 15th century and had a complicated history of ownership until 1649 when it was rendered uninhabitable during the Civil War. It remained a shell until the 19th century when it was bought by the brothers William and John Dent, Worcester glove-makers, who restored it and ensured its survival.

The castle's setting has very much the character of medieval parkland, untouched either by any 17th-century formal arrangement or 18th-century landscaping, because the estate was uninhabited during those key periods in English garden history. Although some of the medieval park walls survive, the garden that visitors may see today is entirely of the 19th and 20th centuries. South-east of the castle the Queen's Garden dates from the restoration by the Dents in the 1850s. It is flanked by wide yew hedges which enclose shady walks and break out into rounded buttresses at each end and in the middle, with 'doors' giving access and 'windows' offering framed views of the gardens. Pairs of immense domed bushes of yew guard each end of the garden and gravel paths thread their way between beds that are edged with finely cut turf. The beds are arranged in a rectilinear, symmetrical pattern with, at their centre, a balustraded pool and fountain. In the 19th century the garden would have had elaborate seasonal bedding schemes but since 1988 it has been replanted with very large numbers of the old-fashioned kinds of shrub roses, making a far decorative but less labour-intensive arrangement. East of the Queen's Garden a raised terrace gives views of the gardens on one side and the parkland beyond the wall to the south. Such raised walks were often made on the edge of parkland in the late middle ages, sometimes incorporating gazebos, to allow the ladies to admire the hunt from a position of comfort and safety.

North-west of the house are the roofless remains of a 15th-century tithe barn with a long rectangular lily pond in front of them. The walls of the barn are generously festooned with roses, wisteria and clematis and more unusual plants such as the trumpet vine *Campsis radicans*. The buildings of the castle itself, of pale Cotswold stone, are visible from every part of the garden, rising up to form a wonderfully romantic backdrop.

RIGHT *The walnut (*Juglans regia*) was probably brought to England by the Romans. This dramatic old specimen makes a fine ornament.*

OPPOSITE *The Victorian parterres, framed in venerable yew hedges, have been given lively new planting. The palest blue* Veronica gentianoides *is in the foreground with, beyond, rosemary, lavender and a profusion of shrub roses.*

Painshill Park

The story of Painshill Park is a rare example of how it is possible for a very famous garden almost entirely to disappear – and yet be brought back to triumphant life.

The creator of the garden was the Hon. Charles Hamilton who bought the land in 1738 and worked on it until 1773 when overwhelming debts forced him to sell. The site he acquired was very poor farmland – 'a most cursed hill' as Horace Walpole described it – but it did have advantages of setting, with slopes running down to the river Mole. Being the youngest son of the Duke of Abercorn's 14 children, Charles Hamilton was by no

and managed to create one of the most remarkable, and most remarked on, of all 18th-century landscape gardens.

Little is known of Hamilton's background, but he had been twice on the Grand Tour and had spent a long time in Italy and France where he immersed himself in the study of art. It is also known that he took an informed interest in plants. His garden is a series of episodes of individual character strung out along the banks of the river and the shores of a lake which he created. Architecture and Arcadian scenes play their part but the distinctive effect of Painshill is due to Hamilton's interest in plants. He introduced

The island grotto is one of the finest surviving examples of an 18th-century grotto. After years of restoration, its true nature is now being revealed in all its splendour.

means able to finance the rich man's game of laying out a great landscape. He scraped along, however, securing the occasional Crown appointment (such as Receiver General of the royal revenues of Minorca)

many exotics, particularly North American evergreens, planting them not as specimens, but in a naturalistic way. John Claudius Loudon in his *Encyclopaedia of Gardening* (1822) describes Painshill as 'one of the most beautiful and meritorious places in England'. He goes on to say: 'The woods were planted so as of themselves to produce variety, by adopting the manner of grouping the natural orders; thus, in one part the pine and fir tribes prevailed, in another, aquatics, and so on'.

The planting seems to have anticipated the kind of natural gardening, paying attention to habitat, which William Robinson was to popularise well over 100 years later.

Hamilton's buildings give very different moods to the various parts of the garden. The airy, open Gothic Temple, built in the 1750s, commands serene views of grazing sheep and placid waters. The Ruined Abbey, however, in low-lying land on the edge of the lake has all the 'horrid gloom' of the Gothic novel.

The Mausoleum, on a loop of the river, was built as a ruined Roman triumphal arch and evokes melancholy feelings of the passing of empires and the decay of earthly things.

From Hamilton's departure in 1773, until World War II, the estate was well maintained, but it then went downhill fast. By 1981, when a trust was set up to restore it, Painshill was all but lost. The trust's achievements have been nothing short of miraculous and Hamilton's mysterious and magical garden has been retrieved from apparent extinction. Many buildings have been restored and work continues. His exotic Turkish Tent (actually made of brick, lead and painted canvas) has just been completed and once again rises on the slopes above the cascade. The extraordinary labyrinthine grotto on its island, created by Joseph Lane of Tisbury in the 1760s, is coming back to dazzling life. Elizabeth Montagu wrote in 1755: 'Pray follow me to Mr Hamilton's. I

The Ruined Abbey on the northern bank of the lake is seen with the newly replanted vineyard behind it. According to Charles Hamilton, in the 18th century it produced wine with 'a finer flavour than the best Champaign'.

must tell you it beggars all description. The art of hiding art is here in such sweet perfection.' Visitors can now follow Elizabeth Montagu and see with their own eyes the nature of Hamilton's genius.

Mount Edgcumbe

CORNWALL

The house at Mount Edgcumbe was built in the 1550s by Sir Richard Edgcumbe but it was almost entirely destroyed by fire in World War II. The present house was built in 1951 to the designs of Adrian Gilbert Scott and is of the same dimensions as the 16th-century mansion. The great thing here, however, is the marvellous site on a cliff with sea-views in one direction and views over Plymouth Sound in another. Since the 17th century visitors have commented on the richly wooded slopes but when the Edgcumbes came here this was a featureless hillside. Celia Fiennes on a visit in 1698 saw a 'hill bedeck'd with woods which are divided into several rows of trees with walks' – an effect which visitors today may clearly see, with a spectacular triple avenue of chestnuts, oaks and sycamores marching down the slopes below the house. One survivor from the earliest planting, a 400-year-old lime tree, can be found behind the house within the Earl's Garden, which is also enhanced by a Lucombe oak (Quercus × hispanica 'Lucombeana'), a rare Mexican pine (Pinus patula) and a striking 18th-century Shell Seat. When John Claudius Loudon came on one of his tree-spotting jaunts in 1842 he saw much to admire – magnolias 9 metres high, numerous cork oaks (Quercus suber, the tender evergreen oak from the Mediterranean – still a great feature here), strawberry trees (Arbutus unedo) 12 metres high and much else.

In the 18th century the estate had been at least partly landscaped, with spectacular winding walks along the very edge of the cliffs between the woods and sea. At the highest point was a viewing terrace made by Lord Edgcumbe before 1750. In 1773 Wedgwood used a 1755 drawing of this terrace, a famous feature of its time, on one of the plates made for Catherine the Great's dinner service. From the same period as Lord Edgcumbe's landscaping activities is a sham

ruin, festooned with suitably romantic ivy, with a soaring tracery window.

North-east of the house on lower ground by the sea a series of formal gardens was made in the late 18th and early 19th centuries, on the site of the former 'wilderness' shown in Badeslade's view of 1737. This area is enclosed by immense hedges of holm oak (Quercus ilex), which Loudon had admired in 1842 and which provide protection from the sea winds. The Italian garden has a handsome conservatory made before 1788, a central pool with a flamboyant fountain and a double balustraded staircase ornamented with statues. A French garden dates from the same period. Nearby is a charming classical style English Garden House which lay at the heart of the earlier wilderness garden, and dates from before 1729. Some of the National Camellia collection can be found close at hand with 20 species and 450 different cultivars, the largest collection in the country.

In 1971 the garden at Mount Edgcumbe was bought by Plymouth City Council and Cornwall County Council to form a country park. More restoration remains to be done but it still preserves great character.

ABOVE *An Ionic temple, built in 1789, carries an inscription from Milton's 'Paradise Lost'. It commands views both over the sea and inwards towards the garden.*

RIGHT *Visitors may experience similar feelings to those expressed by William Beckford in 1781: 'Here I am breathing the soft air of Mount Edgcumbe standing on the brink of a Cliff overlooking the sea and singing Notturnos'.*

Knightshayes Court

'Knightshayes is eminently pictur-esque, executed with great vigour', wrote C. L. Eastlake in his *History of the Gothic Revival*. It was built between 1869 and 1874 to the designs of William Burges, the extraordinary Pre-Raphaelite architect, for John Heathcoat Amory whose family had made a fortune out of lace-making. Burges was famous for his glittering polychromatic interiors but, alas, Heathcoat Amory was not rich enough to complete the house to his designs. From the garden point of view, however, this scarcely matters for the exterior was completed as he intended and its long south façade makes a decorative prospect from the gardens.

The house has a marvellous position with parkland, studded with fine trees, extending southwards towards Tiverton. On this side of the house formal terraces were laid out in the 1870s by Edward Kemp, an influential garden designer and author of *How to Lay out a Small Garden* (1850). These terraces, with central steps leading down to a pool, survive very much as he made them. Dating from the same period as this work is a formal area to the east of the house enclosed in yew hedges. But the true distinction of the garden comes from the work of Sir John and Lady Heathcoat Amory since 1946.

The earth of this part of Devon is a reddish-brown, the same colour as the stone from which Knightshayes Court is built. In this particular site there is the oddity that the soil in the terrace beds is neutral whereas that to the east of the house, in old woodland, is acid. The Heathcoat Amorys developed this area making what they thought of as 'a garden in a wood' rather than merely what is thought of as a woodland garden. Here plants were very carefully chosen for their site, both from the point of view of habitat but also with aesthetic considerations. They thinned out the woodland, planting many ornamental trees and shrubs and opening out glades. There are marvellous magnolias, maples, southern beeches (*Nothofagus* species), the exquisite pale yellow early-flowering *Stachyurus praecox* and many rhododendrons. Much attention is paid to underplanting with several different erythroniums, ferns, waves of blue-bells, wood anemones and in the summer lilies and both blue- and white-flowered willow gentians (*Gentiana asclepiadea*).

The Heathcoat Amorys also introduced distinguished planting in the formal areas closer to the house. The terrace beds in Edward Kemp's day were planned for bed-ding schemes – they now have a fastidious mixed planting. Knightshayes is often thought of as a 'plantsman's garden' but there are parts where simplicity and effectiveness of design rather than plantsmanship is the most striking characteristic. The old yew-enclosed pool garden has a white figure set against crisply clipped yew buttresses and no other planting but a single weeping silver pear (*Pyrus salicifolia* 'Pendula') by the pool, with lilies dappling the surface and a fringe of irises at the edge. Knowing when to plant no more is as important as knowing when, and what, to plant.

Irises and water lilies ornament the waters of a round pond. A weeping silver pear (Pyrus salicifolia 'Pendula') stands out against buttresses of crisp yew.

Abbotsbury Sub-Tropical Gardens

DORSET

For some gardens the single most important factor is the site. Abbotsbury Gardens on the Dorset coast are sited in an exceptionally protected position, on sloping land running down to Chesil Beach. The coastal position, protected by woodland on higher land above, means that temperatures below freezing are uncommon. Much of this woodland consists of planned windbreaks, often of the evergreen holm oak (*Quercus ilex*) which is not only very decorative but provides particularly good protection in winter. Other places on the mainland of Britain are virtually frost-free, such as parts of Cornwall and the west coast of Scotland, but they have a very high rainfall which limits the range of plants that may be grown. At Abbotsbury the rainfall is relatively low, but a high degree of humidity is given by the sea, and a wider range of garden plants may be grown here than in any other garden on the mainland. The fertile soil is sufficiently acid to provide excellent conditions for the great Asiatic flowering shrubs – camellias, magnolias and rhododendrons.

A house was built at Abbotsbury in 1765 by the 1st Countess of Ilchester who also laid out a walled garden. The castle was burnt down in 1913 and its successor was demolished in 1936, but the 18th-century walled garden still survives, as does the astonishing collection of plants that was built up chiefly in the 19th century. The Honourable William Fox-Strangways, later the 4th Earl of Ilchester, who died in 1865, was one of a band of aristocratic plant collectors who introduced into 19th-century England a dazzling stream of new plants. His name is commemorated in the genus *Stranvaesia*, named in his honour by the botanist John Lindley who described him as 'a learned and indefatigable investigator of the

flora of Europe'. In fact, his plant interests extended far beyond Europe; among the plants he introduced to cultivation are *Photinia* (formerly *Stranvaesia*) *nussia* from the Himalayas and the beautiful tender evergreen, autumn-flowering *Citronella mucronata* from Chile. The development of the garden continued throughout the 19th century and by 1899 a plant catalogue shows over 5,000 different plants grown. Subsequently there was a slackening of pace but since the 1960s the gardens have been restored and expanded.

Today the gardens present the appearance of a marvellous jungle where the visitor, at every turn, will discover a rarity or some enchanting prospect. The site, well watered and undulating, has been given an entirely naturalistic appearance with ambling paths threading their way through the exotic foliage. It remains an exceptional collection of plants with unforgettable individual specimens grown to exceptional size – such as a great Caucasian wingnut, *Pterocarya fraxinifolia*, well over 30 metres high, of which the only larger specimen in the country is at the neighbouring Strangways estate of Melbury. Everywhere there are fine trees, with an exceptional collection of dogwoods, inclu-

ding those such as *Cornus capitata* too tender for all but the mildest gardens. The banks of streams are planted with Asiatic primulas, followed in summer by gunnera, petasites and rheum displaying spectacular leaves.

Since the terrible storm damage to the garden in January 1990, a new, 10 year phase of restoration is underway. The rare planting continues, with the addition of species in specific geographical zones such as a Himalayan glade, and New Zealand and South American sites. Abbotsbury is a treasure trove for the botanist, and for the ordinary visitor a place of memorable pleasure.

Chiswick House

'I assure you,' wrote Alexander Pope in 1732, 'Chiswick House has been to me the finest thing this glorious sun has shined on.' The house was designed from 1726 onwards by Richard Boyle, the 3rd Earl of Burlington, and it became a key influence in architectural taste, sparking a craze for Palladianism in England. Lord Burlington had imbibed the essence of Palladio direct, by studying his buildings, especially in Vicenza, and buying his drawings. The lovely domed house at Chiswick was modelled on Palladio's Villa Rotonda. It was built alongside old Chiswick House, a Jacobean manor which was demolished in the late 18th century. Lord Burlington had inherited the title and estates in 1703, at the age of 10, and his first architectural work was a garden house, known as the *casina* or *bagnio*, which was built in 1717. It was flanked by statues of his two heroes, Inigo Jones and Andrea Palladio, which still survive in a new position by the house, although the *bagnio* was demolished in 1778. The garden that existed before the 3rd Earl built his Palladian villa was an elaborate formal confection, typical of its period; John Macky described it in his *A Journey Through England* (1724): 'the Earl of Burlington's fine

Gardens at Chiswick. The whole Contrivance of 'em is the Effect of his Lordship's own Genius, and singular fine Taste. Every Walk terminates with some little Building, one with a Heathen Temple, for instance the Pantheon; another a little villa, where my Lord often dines instead of his House.'

Few gardens have been so comprehensively depicted in their heyday, in paintings, drawings and engravings, as Chiswick. These show the bewildering series of changes either contemplated or achieved. Lord Burlington's idea was to make a garden of the kind that he supposed had existed in the ancient world. In the 1720s William Kent, who had already worked on the house, began to have an influence in the garden. The orange tree garden shown in Rysbrack's painting of c.1728 had a domed temple, like a mini-Pantheon, de-

signed by Kent, a pool with an obelisk and orange trees in tubs arranged on encircling terraces resembling an amphitheatre. Kent's drawings also show ideas for an exedra, a curved wall or hedge embellished with figures. An exedra was certainly made after 1733, and survives, alongside the orange tree garden, with yew hedges and a mixture of statues and urns.

After Lord Burlington's death in 1753 the estate passed by his daughter to the Cavendish family of Chatsworth. The 6th Duke of Devonshire added a conservatory designed by Samuel Ware in 1813 south of which Lewis Kennedy laid out an 'Italian garden' the following year. After being let for some years to tenants, the whole estate was sold in 1929 by the 9th Duke to Middlesex County Council. The grounds are today in the care of the London Borough of Hounslow and the house itself has been transferred to English Heritage. The house has been finely restored and the gardens, retaining much of their old character, are undergoing restoration. Despite being sandwiched between two of the busiest roads in London, both house and garden preserve much of the atmosphere cherished by Lord Burlington.

RIGHT *Old cedars of Lebanon and newly planted Italian cypresses, interspersed with statues and urns, line the path leading from the house to the exedra.*

OPPOSITE *The Italian Garden was made in the early 19th century. The formal layout today has rows of mop-headed acacia (Robinia pseudoacacia 'Umbraculifera') with box-edged borders filled in summer with bedding schemes.*

Scotney Castle

KENT

There are two castles at Scotney, an old and a new, and between them lies an extraordinary picturesque landscape garden. The manor was held in the 12th century by Lambert de Scoteni but by the 14th century, when the old castle was built, it belonged to the Ashburnham family. It passed by marriage to the Darell family who lived here until the estate was sold to Edward Hussey in 1778. His grandson, another Edward, decided to build a new castle, high on a hill above the old one. He chose as his architect Anthony Salvin who, between 1837 and 1844, built a gabled mansion in the Tudor style.

In choosing the site for his new house Hussey consulted William Sawrey Gilpin, an artist and landscape gardener, who believed, in the words of his mentor Sir Uvedale Price, that the 'requisite necessary to form a just taste in landscape… [is] the study of landscape painting in the first instance'. With Gilpin's advice, a picturesque garden was laid out between the two castles which took every advantage of the fine site. The stone for the new castle had been quarried on the slopes below it and the workings created romantic scars and hollows in the land. A viewing terrace was made immediately below the new castle commanding views down the slopes towards the old castle. This, with its battlemented corner tower, romantically moated, and its 17th-century extensions removed, forms the perfect picturesque eye-catcher.

Between the two castles the rocky slopes are planted with ornamental trees and shrubs. This is acid soil and provides excellent conditions for azaleas, rhododendrons and the American mountain laurel, *Kalmia latifolia*, which W. J. Bean describes as 'probably the most beautiful evergreen shrub obtained from that region'. In spring its flowers, ranging from almost white to rosy pink, are a spectacular sight and its glossy foliage is ornamental throughout the year. Today, although there was terrible damage in the great storm of 1987, the plantings are splendidly mature. In spring the flowering shrubs clothe the slopes in colour and later in the year there is the brilliant autumn foliage of *Liquidambar styraciflua*, tupelos (*Nyssa sylvatica*) and many Japanese maples. Evergreen trees such as the American incense cedar (*Calocedrus decurrens*), with its strikingly tall and slender shape, provide distinguished winter ornament.

In the forecourt of the old castle a herb garden surrounding an old well head was laid out by Christopher Hussey shortly after the National Trust took over in 1978. Nearby on a shady peninsula a bronze statue by Henry Moore (given to Scotney by Moore himself in memory of Christopher Hussey) seems strangely at home in its naturalistic setting.

The view from the bastion at Scotney and the descent down the densely planted slopes, with distinguished planting pressing in all about, allowing half-veiled glimpses of the old castle, are marvellous. When the visitor arrives at the waters of the moat and looks back, another treat is in store, for the new castle takes on a different appearance, now rising dramatically among the conifers on the heights above.

From the bastion below the new castle, a picturesque
view of the old castle framed by trees.

Cobham Hall

A balustrade edges the bastion which is the culminating point of Humphry Repton's terrace. From the bastion there are views over the former deer park.

In its day Cobham Hall was one of the finest houses in England and had a garden to match. It was built in the late 16th century of rose-red brick with stone dressings for Lord Cobham, whose family was long established in this corner of Kent – there are Cobham memorials in the nearby church of St Mary Magdalene going back to the early 14th century. The house passed to the Dukes of Lennox and Richmond in the early 17th century and there were many additions to the house. The succession of families involved then becomes exceedingly complicated; by the early 18th century the estate had passed to

the Bligh family who acquired the Earldom of Darnley. In 1962 the house and gardens passed into the ownership of the Westwood Educational Trust for use as a girls' school.

The earliest mention of the garden is contained in Holinshed's *The Chronicles of England, Scotland and Ireland* (1577) in which it is described as 'a rare garden . . . in which no varietie of strange flower and trees do want,

which praise or price maie obtaine from the furthest part of Europe or from other strange Countries, whereby it is not inferior to the garden of Semiramis' – Semiramis was the queen of Assyria who founded Babylon whose hanging gardens were one of the wonders of the ancient world. In the 16th and 17th centuries the house was set in a deer park and there is evidence of terracing to the north and south which suggests that there were formal gardens, possibly contemporary with the house. West of the house there were quadruple lime avenues of which a few trees survive to the south-west.

The great event in the history of the garden was the commissioning in 1790 of Humphry Repton to do new designs which are contained in the 'Red Book' which he made for Cobham. Here he describes its future appearance as he saw it in his mind's eye: 'The house is no longer a huge pile standing naked on a vast grazing ground. Its walls are enriched with roses and jasmines: its apartments are perfumed with odours from flowers surrounding it on every side . . . all around is neatness, elegance and comfort.' He created a new curving entrance from the north, removed most of the formal avenues,

Lady Darnley's garden, part of Humphry Repton's work at the end of the 18th century, is embellished with scattered sarsen stones and a dapper Ionic temple.

added an 'irregular flower garden' and planted many trees – of which several magnificent cedars of Lebanon (*Cedrus libani libani*) survive. North of the house, on undulating land, he made informal walks with carefully orchestrated views of James Wyatt's distant mausoleum (1783) and of 'Peggy Taylor's Hill' glimpsed through an opening made in a hedge. The 'irregular flower garden' – Lady

Darnley's garden – had an aviary, a curious grotto called Merlin's Cave, and a beautiful little Ionic temple by Sir William Chambers (1777), which was moved here from Ingess Abbey in 1820. On the far side of the south lawn Repton placed an ornamental dairy, designed by James Wyatt in 1795, to act as an eye-catcher.

Cobham Hall is one of Repton's finest and most elaborate surviving landscapes. There is a programme of restoration afoot but resources are severely limited and progress is necessarily slow. It deserves all the support it can get – few gardens are more worthy of it.

Kiftsgate Court

GLOUCESTERSHIRE

The 20th-century term 'plantsman's garden' too often describes an essentially rather dull place in which the rarity of a plant, or its botanical 'interest', takes precedence over all other considerations. Some gardens, however, manage to accommodate an immense range of good plants in a satisfying design – Kiftsgate Court is an admirable example, where over a long period successive members of a single family have made a striking contribution.

The house was built in the 1880s incorporating an 18th-century portico from nearby Mickleton Manor. It lies on the very brim of the Cotswold escarpment, with the ground sloping very sharply away from the house to the north-west, affording beautiful views over the Vale of Evesham. The estate was bought in 1917 by Mr and Mrs J. B. Muir and it was Mrs Muir, better known as Heather Muir, who made the garden from 1920 onwards. Kiftsgate is the neighbouring estate to Hidcote Manor where Lawrence Johnston, a friend of Mrs Muir's, had been making his famous garden before World War I.

This is a very exposed site, taking the full brunt of the wind sweeping across from the west. Mrs Muir planted windbreaks and gradually enshrouded the immediate surroundings of the house with protective plantings which, together with the excellent

The sunken White Garden has a fountain at the centre made of an old well-head. In the foreground is the yellow Rosa ecae and in the background the decorative foliage of peonies, Cornus controversa 'Variegata', Cercis siliquastrum and Hydrangea villosa.

natural frost drainage, have created the best possible micro-climate in this cold part of England. Her daughter, Mrs D. H. Binny, continued the development of the garden and her daughter, Mrs A. H. Chambers, now maintains the tradition.

The garden today is an admirable mixture of formality and informality. Near the house, formal enclosures – Four Squares and the White Garden – are intimately linked with

the architecture of the house. North-east of them, the rose garden, enclosed in beech hedges, has a path with hedges of *Rosa gallica* 'Versicolor' and on either side very deep borders of shrub roses. Heather Muir was one of the pioneer rediscoverers of old roses and also the introducer of new ones: the giant climbing *R. filipes* 'Kiftsgate' was first grown here – the original plant flourishes – and the exquisite *R.* 'Heather Muir' (a seedling of *R. sericea*) may still be seen in the White Garden. On the slopes of 'The Banks' south-west of the house, Mrs Muir made zigzagging paths, using the tops of old staddle stones (once used for supporting barns to keep rats from the grain). Here, in a sharply drained position protected by trees, a very different range of plants is grown, some of them very tender. Here are olearias from New Zealand, cistus from the Mediterranean and ceanothus from California. At the very foot of the slope, in the sunny Lower Garden, are abutilons, scented *Azara dentata* from Chile, tender *Buddleja fallowiana* and the lovely red-stemmed *Drimys lanceolata*.

The overwhelming atmosphere at Kiftsgate is one of abundance. But this is no modish jungle in which neglect is made a virtue. It is rather a richly planted landscape in which the hand of the gardener and artist is firmly present but never flaunted.

A virtuoso arrangement of red and purple beneath the pillared portico: in the foreground are rich purple and rosy pink penstemons with more substantial cerise pink lavatera, abelia and Rosa glauca in the background.

The Manor House, Upton Grey

HAMPSHIRE

There has in recent years been a tremendous renaissance of interest in the garden ideas of Gertrude Jekyll – her books have been reprinted and many books about her have been published. Although she died as recently as 1932, she had the misfortune to have been at the peak of her activity before World War I – just before the catastrophic social and economic unheavals that all but destroyed the professionally maintained middle-class gardens which were her most characteristic work. In her lifetime she designed a very large number of gardens and advised on many others, yet almost none has been continuously kept up to show us the true nature of her genius. However, the scholarly study of her ideas, now extremely well documented, has permitted accurate recreations of her gardens, of which Upton Grey is a first-class example.

The house and garden at Upton Grey are a shrine to the Arts and Crafts movement. They were bought in 1905 by Charles Holme, the editor of *The Studio*, who com-

RIGHT *Looking back towards the house from the formal terraces, the Arts and Crafts house is seen through a haze of planting. The house and garden both display a respect for traditional materials and craftsmanship.*

OPPOSITE *The lower terrace of Gertrude Jekyll's formal garden is edged on three sides by drystone walling blurred with her characteristic planting of hart's tongue ferns, aubrieta, blue and white* Campanula carpatica, *lavender and* Arenaria montana. *These planted walls envelop the visitor in colour, scent and form.*

missioned a complete rebuilding of the old house from the architect Ernest Newton. Between 1908 and 1909 Gertrude Jekyll prepared plans for a new garden. She was then at the apogee of her career, fresh from one of her finest commissions in collaboration with Sir Edwin Lutyens – Hestercombe in Somerset. The scale of activities at Upton Grey was more modest but it was nevertheless one of her best creations. Like so many other gardens of the period, it did not survive the two World Wars and when the present owners, John and Rosamund Wallinger, bought the estate in 1984 the garden had virtually disappeared. Luckily, however, the original planting plans survived and, with the help of Hampshire County Council, the Gardens Trust and

experts on historic gardens, they have been able to carry out a remarkable reconstruction.

To the front of the house Miss Jekyll laid out a garden of naturalistic informality in the style of William Robinson, with grass, winding paths, a pool and ornamental trees and shrubs. On the other side of the house she contrived an intricate, but unforced, formal arrangement of three terraces linked by stone steps with 'wings' on either side of the upper terrace providing varied views of the planting in the lower terraces. Retaining dry-stone walls are planted in characteristic Jekyllian fashion with, among a wide variety of plants, hart's tongue ferns (*Asplenium scolopendrium*), valerian (*Centranthus ruber*) and fumitory (*Corydalis lutea*). A pergola draped with roses, summer jasmine and *Aristolochia macrophylla*

runs down the centre of the first terrace drawing the eye away from the house. Below, on the second terrace, eight trapezoidal beds have balanced plantings of pink double peonies (*Paeonia lactiflora* 'Sarah Bernhardt') and four 19th-century roses which include 'Madame Caroline Testout' in the very rare bush form. This rose has equally voluptuous flowers as the peonies, is richly scented and of similar colouring. The beds are edged in silver lambs' lugs (*Stachys byzantina*) – a favourite Jekyll device.

The subtle changes of level, beautiful details of stonework, restful symmetry, and bold, unpretentious planting are all typical of Miss Jekyll. Upton Grey, now impeccably restored, is one of the best places to understand the essence of her art.

Cliveden

BERKSHIRE

The site of Cliveden is spectacular, as John Evelyn recorded in his diary in 1679 – 'Cliefden that stupendious natural Rock, Wood & prospect of the Duke of Buckinghams'. George Villiers, 2nd Duke of Buckingham had bought the estate shortly after the restoration of the monarchy, attracted by its position high up on chalk cliffs above the Thames whose 'serpentining' at this point Evelyn especially admired. It is clear that this position was also appreciated by the Duke of Buckingham who built an arcaded viewing terrace, 30 metres long, designed by the architect William Winde, commanding the best views down the wooded slopes towards the river. On the Duke's death, the estate was sold to the Earl of Orkney who himself laid out the formal gardens whose design has a powerful influence on the appearance of the gardens today. Charles Bridgeman was employed to make yew walks on the slopes west of the house and a turf amphitheatre which, in 1740, was the scene of the first performance of Thomas Arne's masque *Alfred* which contains the anthem 'Rule Britannia'.

Lord Orkney commissioned a parterre from Claude Desgots, a nephew of André le Nôtre, whose original drawings, dated 1713, survive. These, sent from Versailles, show two possibilities to replace the existing parterre which had probably been designed by Henry Wise. Neither was executed – Lord Orkney chose something much simpler, what he described as a 'quaker' parterre, a rectangular lawn with raised walks. The present design of beds dates from the 1850s when Sir Charles Barry was working on a new classical house to replace the previous one which had been destroyed by fire in 1849. This pattern of long wedge-shaped box hedges remains today but in its heyday, under the head gardener John Fleming, it was the scene of influential experiments in elaborate seasonal bedding schemes – which involved on one occasion 30,000 plants of which 10,000 were tulips.

An account of these experiments was published in Fleming's book *Spring and Winter Gardening* (1864). The parterre today is planted with a simple but effective arrangement, following the original outlines, of blocks of santolina, senecio and nepeta.

In 1893 the estate was bought by William Waldorf Astor (later 1st Viscount Astor) who, as he was to do also at Hever Castle, used his collection of classical antiquities and architectural fragments to embellish the grounds. At Cliveden, apart from magnificent Roman sarcophagi, these notably included the superb early 17th-century balustrades bought (against the wishes of the Italian government) by W. W. Astor from the Villa Borghese in Rome. These were re-erected round William Winde's viewing terrace. The Italian influence is also evident in the Long Garden north of the house where 18th-century Venetian statues of figures from the *commedia dell'arte* – Pantaleone, Arlechino and so on – are disposed about slender box-edged beds with flamboyant yew topiary.

Among the most distinguished and attractive features at Cliveden are the herbaceous borders which face each other across the huge entrance court. These were designed in 1969 by Graham Thomas for the National Trust which now owns the estate. They are planted in interweaving drifts of colour according to Mr Thomas' adaptation of Gertrude Jekyll's theories on colour in the garden: 'One border has got no pinks, mauves or purples, the other has got no oranges, reds, or yellows; and that, I think, is the way to do gardens.'

ABOVE *A glimpse of the Thames through the woods on the slopes below the garden.*

OPPOSITE *In the Long Garden a stone Venetian statue of a* commedia dell'arte *figure is echoed by a tall clipped yew. The box hedge below forms a sinuous ribbon.*

Seaton Delaval Hall

NORTHUMBERLAND

Sir John Vanbrugh designed Seaton Delaval Hall, which was built for Admiral George Delaval, between 1720 and 1728. Vanbrugh – soldier, playwright, architect and garden designer – was one of the most extraordinary figures in an extraordinary age. The house at Seaton Delaval was one of his very last works, only completed after his death in 1726.

The site for the Admiral's new house was both dramatic and appropriate – on the Northumberland coast hard by Whitley Bay. The house that Vanbrugh designed is magnificently theatrical, rearing up on its open site, its dark stone frequently shrouded in sea mist. Just as Vanbrugh was so adept at designing great garden buildings – such as those he made at Castle Howard or at Claremont – so he was always aware of the role of the house itself as an ingredient in the landscape. It is not known what gardening works Vanbrugh executed at Seaton Delaval but some traces from his time do survive. An avenue south-west of the house almost certainly dates from the 1720s. Within the garden, to the west of the house, there are traces of earth bastions of exactly the type found in English formal gardens of the early 18th century. There is evidence that the land was built up on three sides of the house to form a great platform.

The Delavals were an unlucky family. The Admiral died before the Hall was finished and his heir Francis Blake Delaval fell down dead under the portico of the house in 1752. The last Delaval died in 1814 and the estate passed to the Astley family whose descendant, the 22nd Lord Hastings, lives there today. A disastrous fire in 1822 gutted the greater part of the house and it is only under the present owner that the house has been made good, with a new roof and new windows exactly matching the old. The main part of the house, however, is a shell, none of the interiors having been restored.

Lord Hastings has taken a great interest in the garden, laying out in 1947 a new formal garden to the west of the house, to the designs of James Russell. Here is a rose parterre, enclosed in low box hedges, and overlooked by a fine lead statue of Samson slaying the Philistine. On lower ground, passing through a set of magnificent early 18th-century wrought-iron gates, James Russell made a stately arrangement of swirling box hedge compartments filled with blocks of santolina, 'sentry boxes' of clipped yew, and a procession of stone urns down each side. At the centre is a modern, Italianate fountain. At the far end, on a grassy eminence above one of the early 18th-century bastions, a lone statue of the goddess Diana stands out against woodland.

Behind the house a beautiful old weeping ash, *Fraxinus excelsior* 'Pendula', shades a gravel path which curves round to follow a pair of sweeping mixed borders of modern planting. From this point a distant obelisk may be glimpsed in the old parkland south of the house. Attractive as the garden and its various ornaments are, the eye is irresistibly drawn to Vanbrugh's prodigious house.

ABOVE *In the formal garden designed by James Russell, urns are surrounded by mounds of clipped santolina and enclosed in circular box-edged beds. A procession of 'sentry boxes' of clipped yew appear behind the borders.*

RIGHT *The modern rose garden, with bedding roses, is designed as a formal parterre in keeping with the formality of the house which rises above it. In the background Samson is glimpsed slaughtering a Philistine.*

Cottesbrooke Hall

ottesbrooke Hall was built for Sir John Langham very early in the 18th century, possibly to the designs of Francis Smith of Warwick. It is built of fine rose-pink brick enriched with pale Ketton stone and is of exquisite refinement. It is one of the candidates, and certainly not the least likely, as the original of Jane Austen's Mansfield Park. In the 1770s there were additions to the house which included bows at either end and handsome lodges and a screen with Coadestone detailing at the western entrance. There were further changes between the wars, when the house was turned back to front and Lord Gerald Wellesley designed a new entrance in the north façade, with the former entrance becoming the garden side of the house. The south side was then brilliantly embellished with stately formal gardens designed by Geoffrey Jellicoe in 1937.

Nothing is known of the early history of the garden, but a striking feature of the house is that it is aligned on the distant spire – three miles away in an elevated position – of All Saints church, Brixworth. There are signs on this, the south side of the house, of a designed landscape, quite probably made when the house was built, one of whose vistas 'borrowed' the spire as a focal point.

The true distinction of the garden, however, belongs almost entirely to the 20th century. Between 1911 and 1914 (when the estate was leased by Captain Robert Brassey) the Arts and Crafts architect Robert Weir Schultz worked on the garden and laid out a rose garden with an elaborate pergola south-west of the house. After World War I, in the Hon. Lady Macdonald-Buchanan's time, many changes took place and it was she who gave the garden its present character. She removed the pergola in the present pool garden and commissioned an elegant pillared pavilion designed by Dame Sylvia Crowe.

In the walled garden, with its Arts and Crafts character, lead putti ornament a pool flanked by tubs of variegated Abutilon pictum variegatum.

The planting here was enriched with fine magnolias and, by the pavilion, a *Carpenteria californica* looks surprisingly healthy in this not very balmy part of the country. Running west from the house is a pair of virtuoso mixed borders on either side of a paved path, partly overshadowed in dramatic fashion by superlative cedars of Lebanon (*Cedrus libani libani*). South of this, the statue walk announces a more sombre atmosphere; here a broad grassy walk leads past a yew hedge, breaking out occasionally into buttresses and

The south façade of the house with its refined formal garden – impeccable yew topiary, bushes of perpetual-flowering 'Iceberg' roses and tubs of brilliant blue agapanthus – make a distinguished background to statues.

ornamented with a series of magnificent statues by Peter Scheemakers. A handsome urn, designed by Lord Gerald Wellesley, is aligned with the path and serves as an eye-catcher backed by woodland.

The gardens immediately alongside the

house are varied in atmosphere but they are all formal in spirit. The wild garden, westwards across the park, is a beautiful woodland garden with distinguished maples and rhododendrons and many moisture-loving herbaceous plants relishing the banks of a brook – astilbes, hostas, ligularias, primulas and much else contribute to a brilliant, but naturalistic, spring and summer picture. Cottesbrooke Hall is still privately owned and both house and gardens are looked after to perfectionist standards.

Mannington Hall

*T*here are very few houses in England to match Mannington Hall for irresistible charm. Built of Norfolk flint, with tall chimney stacks rising above its crenellated walls, it seems to float peacefully on its moat. It was built in the 15th century for a kinsman of the great Paston family and passed later into the possession of the Walpole family who lived at Mannington only intermittently, preferring their main estate of Wolterton nearby. In the middle of the 19th century Horatio Walpole, the 4th Earl of Orford, Gothicised the house even further and added misogynist inscriptions in Gothic lettering – 'Trust your bark to the winds, do not trust your heart to girls. For the wave is safer than a woman's heart.' He, too, added

the picturesque antiquarian fragments to the grounds of the ruined Saxon church that stands near the hall.

The moated island has had a garden since the 16th century but its appearance today dates from the 19th century when the banks of the moat were partly hedged in yew. In the main part of the garden to the west of the hall, the entrance drive, called The Avenue, existed in 1742 when a survey of the estate was made. It has been given greater emphasis by the addition of lime trees in the 1970s.

From a horticultural point of view the greatest interest of Mannington is the developments undertaken since 1969 by Lord Walpole. In the process of restoring the garden within the moat, he has added a

ABOVE *In the moated garden a bust is underplanted with bedding roses.*

RIGHT *The moated island is the site of the oldest part of the garden. The waters are decorated by lilies and modern roses stand out against yew hedges.*

garden of modern roses and a scented garden. Beyond the moat, in a walled former kitchen garden, he introduced an entirely new feature in 1982, the Heritage Rose Garden. Here he benefited from the help and advice of the rose nurseryman Peter Beales whose nursery is not far away at Attleborough. Peter Beales has probably the largest collection of old roses in commercial cultivation in the country and was able to supply many cultivars which are very hard to find. Roses do particularly well in the cold but sunny climate of north Norfolk – cooler temperatures extend the flowering season and keep many diseases at

The dark waters of the moat are enlivened with water lilies, and a weeping willow falls over the walls.

bay. The Heritage Rose Garden has been laid out to show characteristic roses of various periods in appropriate settings. It is a vivid demonstration of the history of horticultural fashion, enabling the visitor to see that most garden roses are of very recent introduction. For example, in the middle ages, apart from wild roses such as the dog rose (*R. canina*) or sweet briar (*R. eglanteria*), there were very few others available – the 'Apothecary's Rose', *R. gallica* var. *officinalis* was known in

the 13th century and the Alba rose 'Great Maiden's Blush' was known in the 15th century – and all were graceful plants with quiet colours. At Mannington, with roses grouped historically, the visitor sees how the bright colours (particularly orange) and the huge flowers of many roses are of very recent origin.

Mannington is a romantic place but, apart from the beauty of the site, there is little of garden interest before the 20th-century additions. It is an admirable example of an old garden that has been given an appropriate new life by enterprising owners.

Cragside House

Cragside was the creation of Sir William Armstrong, later Baron Armstrong of Cragside, who made a gigantic fortune out of armaments. During the Crimean War he invented a long-rifled field gun, breech-loading and firing a shell instead of a ball, and the Armstrong gun became the most famous small-arm in the world. In the 1860s he started buying land in the picturesque but desolate Coquet valley and commissioned a house on a virgin site from the architect Norman Shaw. This fantasy house, turreted and towered, made of stone and half-timbering, Gothic and vernacular, in the words of the architectural historian Mark Girouard 'grew enormous in all directions'. Armstrong was in the grip of a land-buying frenzy and by the time of his death in 1900 he had also acquired the ancient estate of Bamburgh Castle on the coast and altogether about 30,000 acres of land. Armstrong filled his house with the latest wonders of applied science – it was the first to be properly lit by electricity and had a hydraulic lift and hydraulically powered spit among many other marvels of gadgetry some of which, as we shall see, extended to the gardens.

Armstrong set about making his gardens with the same unstoppable energy that he devoted to all his activities. The immediate pleasure grounds eventually extended to approximately 1,700 acres, and making the land fertile was an immense task. It is said that Armstrong paid locals a penny for every bucket of fertile soil which they carried to improve the ground in remote stony corners. He planted rhododendrons *en masse* so that the *Gardener's Magazine* reported in 1892 'several hundred thousand have been planted…forming impenetrable thickets, and blooming so profusely as to light up the whole hillside with their varied colours'. There was rock-moving on a grand scale to make the giant rock garden which tumbles down the ravine below the house, with the Debdon Burn at the bottom. On the banks of

the burn he made a pinetum and spanned the waters with an arched bridge of cast-iron.

A great range of glasshouses provided controlled environments for ferns, fruit and cutting plants for the house. The fruit house had hand-operated turntables so that the trees in their pots could be orientated to ensure even growth and to allow the fruit to ripen fully all over the plant. This has recently been restored and is being used to grow fruit cultivars of Armstrong's time.

A picture postcard dating from before World War I shows the Carpet Gardens on sloping beds below the glasshouses. The original patterns of these beds included mathematical puzzles appropriate for a man of science. These have been magnificently

restored in a star and diamond pattern of the 1890s, planted with foliage plants – sempervivums, sedums and creeping senecio among them – which are clipped to give the required smooth carpet-like surface.

Cragside was passed to the National Trust in 1977 but the Trust only took over the main part of the gardens in 1991. Much restoration has already been done and garden taste, rather slower to change than taste in architecture, has rediscovered the charms of Victorian gardening displayed so splendidly here.

The Debdon Burn falls into a dramatic cascade at Cragside Gorge. William Armstrong dammed the burn to provide hydraulic power for all kinds of machinery for the house and garden.

Bramdean House

HAMPSHIRE

The gentlemanly house dates from the early 18th century and is finely built of patterned brick, embellished with a bold hood over the front door supported on carved brackets. Although the house is on a very busy main road, the garden on its far side to the north preserves an atmosphere of ordered, rural calm. The layout here is of unusual historic interest for, although the planting is almost entirely modern, the design is a rare survival of an intimate formal scheme dating from about the same period as the house.

A series of linked gardens, threaded together along an axis that is aligned with the garden door of the house, rises up a gentle hill. The lowest terrace has a circular pool surrounded by paving from which a grass path leads between lavish herbaceous borders planted to provide a continuity of interest from spring deep into autumn. On either side of these borders the planting gives way to less formal arrangements and a fine background of mature trees, chiefly beech and lime. Steps lead up to wrought-iron gates which pierce the wall surrounding the second terrace in which a kitchen garden is combined with ornamental planting. The path, fringed with perennial carnations, continues up the centre with roses on either side arranged in triangular divisions within the beds. A second path runs across the central axis, with screens of clipped yew where they meet, dividing the area into four, and behind the flower beds there is an orderly arrangement of fruit and vegetables. At the far side of this area, enclosed in high brick walls, a further wrought-iron gate leads out to an orchard with flowering cherries, underplanted with immense swathes of daffodils, and an avenue of Irish yews (*Taxus baccata* 'Hibernica'). At the end of the path a very decorative 18th-century summerhouse, crowned with a belfry, faces southwards down towards the gardens and serves as a terminal eye-catcher for the central vista. Passing under a beautiful ash

(*Fraxinus excelsior*) to one side of the summerhouse, the visitor enters a garden of very different character. Here are excellent ornamental trees and shrubs – some very unusual, such as the beautiful Chilean evergreen tree, *Maytenus boaria* – planted in the grassy slopes that skirt the eastern edge of the walled garden and lead back towards the house.

Mrs Wakefield's parents came here during World War II and, although they inherited the fine layout of the garden and some excellent mature trees, the quality of the planting today dates from their and their daughter's time. Here in the chalky soil of the Hampshire Downs they have grown an immense range of plants, making the very best use of all the virtues of the original well-thought-out layout which connects so explicitly with the house. This strong framework prevents the lavish planting dissolving into an incoherent muddle and provides an admirable model from which all gardeners might learn and profit.

ABOVE *In late summer the herbaceous borders that frame the vista from the back of the house take on a blowsy air, contrasting with the crisp classicism of the house. Steps leading to the garden door are given emphasis by rounded ramparts of clipped box.*

RIGHT *From the back of the house a central axis links the various garden compartments, rising gently towards the summerhouse at the brow of the hill. The door is painted a striking almost turquoise blue – an excellent colour for garden woodwork.*

Chelsea Physic Garden

The physic garden, or garden of medicinal plants, is one of the most ancient of all types of garden. Monasteries often had them, and the word *officinalis* found in plant names refers to the monastery *officina* where medicaments were stored. Chelsea Physic Garden was founded by the Worshipful Company of Apothecaries in 1673 on the banks of the Thames in what was then the rural calm of Chelsea. It quickly became one of the great centres of plant studies in England, attracting many of the central figures in botany. Sir Hans Sloane, who owned Chelsea Manor House and was Sir Isaac Newton's successor as President of the Royal Society, was deeply involved with the Physic Garden. When the great Linnaeus, who devised the modern system of plant nomenclature, first visited England in 1736, Sloane was the very first person on whom he paid a call.

It was as a result of Sloane's patronage that in 1722 Philip Miller was appointed Gardener at the Physic Garden where he remained for almost 50 years. Miller built up the international reputation of the garden and was the author of one of the most influential gardening books of the 18th century, *The Gardener's Dictionary* (first published in 1731), which he dedicated to Sir Hans Sloane. Miller's work at Chelsea embraced both practical horticulture – he was a pioneer in the use of the greenhouse and the germination of tropical seeds under heat – as well as more purely botanical problems such as the mechanics of pollination. Through Miller there was an important relationship with the Pennsylvania botanist John Bartram, thanks to whom a stream of North American plants came to Chelsea. Bartram's chief English contact was Peter Collinson who introduced plants to Britain from all over the temperate world. In 1751 he introduced the tree of heaven (*Ailanthus altissima*) from China to the Chelsea Physic Garden.

The 18th century was the period of greatest importance for the Physic Garden. Today, however, it has found a lively new role. It is still a botanical research institute, cultivating a very wide range of medicinal plants and maintaining links with university departments of pharmacology and with the pharmaceutical industry. It is also the first botanic garden in the country to have a garden devoted to plants used medicinally by the world's tribal and indigenous peoples. It involves itself with a gardening school and with the environmental education of school children, and takes an interest in the conservation of garden plants – it holds the National Collection of Cistus.

To the visitor, Chelsea Physic Garden is one of the most beautiful and surprising gardens in London. Its 3.8 acres in walled seclusion give a home to an astonishing range of plants. The micro-climate is very benign, allowing the cultivation of a substantial olive tree (*Olea europaea*) and the prolific flowering of plants, such as the South African *Melianthus major*, that in other places may merely survive. The marvellous old trees and old pattern of order beds, with plants grouped according to their botanical relationships, present a beguiling sight. It is easy to appreciate the rare secret garden atmosphere here; but it is also a place that continues to stimulate a passionate and informed interest in the life of plants.

Painswick Rococo Garden

*M*ost gardens share characteristics with others laid out in the same tradition. Painswick, however, is the sole example of a style of garden known only from paintings and its survival is due to an act of resuscitation that took place long after it had seemed lost for ever.

Painswick House was built in 1730 for Charles Hyett, a lawyer from an old Gloucestershire family. It has an elevated site commanding fine views, from which it derived its original name 'Buenos Aires'. The garden was laid out by Benjamin Hyett between 1738 and 1748. The great travelling priest Bishop Pococke visited it in 1757 and wrote: 'We came to Painswick…just above it Mr Hyett built an house of hewn stone, in a fine situation, and made a very pretty garden…on an hanging ground from the house in a vale'. The house and garden were painted by Thomas Robins in 1748 and the painting survives to this day at Painswick House. Robins was a local artist, born near Cheltenham, one of whose specialities was views of gardens, exquisitely painted and usually embellished with borders of foliage, shells, birds and flowers. The gardens he painted had much in common and have been

described as 'Rococo'; they show a type of intimate landscape garden, ornamented with picturesque buildings and ornaments. His painting of Painswick, with its eccentric perspective, does indeed show a 'hanging' garden in a valley just as described by Bishop Pococke. An exhibition of Robins' paintings in 1976 stimulated interest in his work and garden historians began to explore the places he depicted. As a result, the owners of the garden at Painswick, Lord and Lady Dickinson, realised that below the undergrowth there lay the bones of the garden almost exactly as shown in the Robins painting.

In 1984 Lord and Lady Dickinson embarked on an ambitious programme of restoration. The area had been used partly as a vegetable garden and, in addition, many young trees had been planted. Bulldozers cleared the ground and repeated archaeological digs revealed, just below the surface,

OPPOSITE *The fish pond with the Red House just glimpsed in the background.*

BELOW *The newly reconstructed Exedra seen with a rusticated Doric seat on the left.*

the old pattern of paths and the position of other features. Some of the buildings survived but their relation with each other, and their position in the context of the whole garden, had become completely obscured. Robins' painting is so highly detailed that it served as an essential reference in the recreation of features that had been completely lost. The assumption that Robins depicted the garden as it was actually built has been largely confirmed by the archaeological findings.

Today after more than 10 years' work the visitor may see the garden very closely resembling what Robins painted. It lies concealed in its valley, with paths winding down the well-wooded slopes. Decorative buildings – the Gothic Eagle House and Red House, and the filigree Exedra – punctuate the scene and mark viewing points for the beauties of the garden. Compared with the resounding symphony of a Stourhead or a Stowe, Painswick is intimate chamber music. It is one of the best, and most worthwhile, garden restorations ever undertaken. It is also worth noting that this was carried out not by some great public institution but by a private trust set up for the purpose by Lord and Lady Dickinson.

Tintinhull House

SOMERSET

All good gardens display principles from which ordinary gardeners may learn. Many of those that are open to the public, however, are so dauntingly large that few visitors are able to extract from them the essential ideas that underlie their design. The relatively modest scale of Tintinhull House allows the lessons of excellent design to be demonstrated in an unusually accessible way.

The house, which is not open to the public, was built in about 1600 but was transformed around 1700 by the addition of a very decorative new west front. This, built of warm tawny-brown Ham Hill stone, is classical in inspiration, with a pediment and pilasters, but retains the traditional stone transom windows of the vernacular tradition. Because of its size, this is not the type of house which in the past would have had an especially distinguished garden. To the best of our knowledge it is not until the 20th century that ornamental gardening became important at Tintinhull.

In about 1900 the house was bought by the Rev. Dr S. J. M. Price. To the west of the house, which had originally been the entrance side, he laid out a sequence of enclosed gardens linked by a single axis. This arrangement, very much in the tradition of the Arts and Crafts gardeners of the day, is simple and very effective. It gives the possibility of plantings of different character in the various compartments, yet the whole is made harmonious by being linked together.

In 1933 the house and garden were bought by Captain and Mrs Reiss who were expert gardeners, having already had long experience in a large garden in Gloucestershire.

They developed the garden to the north so that the whole area (including the house) occupied a single enclosed rectangle divided into compartments of different character. Phyllis Reiss was not only a discerning plantswoman but also a gardener of great talent. She made a formal pool garden which could serve as an excellent model for a whole garden design. It consists of a long narrow pool with a pillared summerhouse at its head and strips of lawn and borders on either side. The borders were planned by Mrs Reiss with 'hot' colours – red, yellow and orange – on one side and cool colours – blue, purple, white – on the other. The principles have been maintained although subtly modified and improved by Penelope Hobhouse when she lived here as a tenant of the National Trust in the 1980s.

The whole area of the garden is only 1½ acres, but because of the many compartments and the range of garden styles represented, it seems much larger. Although there is a vast number of different plants and the planting is dense in many areas, there is no feeling of claustrophobia. Vistas lead the eye to other sections, and openings in walls or hedges beckon. Except for a woodland garden (although there are woodland garden effects here), almost every kind of contemporary style of gardening is displayed including a marvellous kitchen garden – not some modish *potager*, but a highly productive space with ornamental planting crowding in all about. Throughout the garden there are excellent plants to admire but its truly exceptional quality is the strength, simplicity and effectiveness of its layout.

Pink musk mallows (Malva moschata) *and the rose 'Mevrouw Nathalie Nypels' edge a stone path leading across the kitchen garden into the pool garden.*

Thorp Perrow Arboretum

NORTH YORKSHIRE

The private collection of plants, especially of trees, is a distinctive type of English garden. It is a curiosity of the climate that, although there is a relatively small number of native plants, only 33 trees for example, the temperate climate will provide a habitat for an immense number of plants from every continent. Indeed, there are probably more garden plants in cultivation in England than in any other country in the world. With this priceless advantage of climate, the temptation to grow a wide range of plants is irresistible. In the first half of the 19th century, when new plants were arriving in bewildering quantity, many collections were started. At Thorp Perrow in the 1840s Lady Augusta Milbank, whose family had been here since the 17th century, made a pinetum, taking particular advantage of the recent introductions from the west coast of North America. Several survivors of her plantings still give much character to the north-west banks of the lake, including such trees as *Pinus ponderosa* which was planted in 1845, the first seeds having arrived in England from the Rocky Mountains in 1826.

The present fame of the arboretum is due to Sir Leonard Ropner who from 1926 until his death in 1977 added immensely to the collection, having taken over very shortly after his father had bought the estate. The site is a flat one and rather windswept, but the density of planting now provides many sheltered parts. Although this is pre-eminently a collection of plants, the space is divided by winding walks and the occasional bold vista such as that which runs from the Rotunda, erected in memory of Sir Leonard by his son, through the woodland, across the lake to the bow-fronted façade of the house.

Trees are strongly emphasised here but there are excellent collections of shrubs and not all these have a particularly botanical bias – a very large collection of garden cultivars of the common lilac (*Syringa vulgaris*), for example, is of special interest to gardeners, as is a delightful collection of laburnums which are grouped together to form a dazzling walk. Furthermore, some of the largest collections of a single genus, such as that of the rowans (*Sorbus* species), happen to contain many brilliant ornamental trees suitable for any garden such as the beautiful little Chinese whitebeam *S. folgneri*.

Plants are generally grouped according to genus but there are also successful thematic arrangements such as the Silver Glade in which plants with silver-grey or gold foliage are grouped together. The Lime Avenue is quite unlike the avenues to be seen marching to the front of many country houses. This one is composed of several different species and among them is a specimen of the Mongolian lime (*Tilia mongolica*) which is among the two or three largest grown in the country.

In more recent years the arboretum has become involved in conservation and is the holder of four collections on behalf of the National Council for the Conservation of Plants and Gardens: ashes (*Fraxinus* species); oaks (*Quercus* species); walnuts (*Juglans* species) and limes (*Tilia* species). The great tree expert Alan Mitchell says of Thorp Perrow that it is 'among the foremost collections in the world'. Botanists can go to marvel but gardeners will also find it enthralling.

ABOVE *The foliage of the smoke-bush* Cotinus coggygria *takes on fine autumn colours*.

OPPOSITE *The pale stems of the ornamental Himalayan raspberry* Rubus biflorus *surrounded by the golds and reds of the autumn foliage of maples*.

Leonardslee

The Sussex landscape has inspired the creation of many woodland gardens. It is partly that the acid soil is favourable for the cultivation of so many ornamental shrubs, but also that the old woodland, and often a dramatic lie of the land, provide a magnificent setting for exotic planting. In the Weald much of the woodland is very ancient – the Domesday Book shows a greater concentration here than in any other part of England, and much of it still survives. St Leonard's Forest, although not far from Gatwick Airport and the creeping suburbia of Crawley, preserves much old woodland and a wonderfully secret character. The garden of Leonardslee takes its name from the forest, and the splendid setting here has inspired gardeners for several generations. When the estate was sold to William Egerton Hubbard in 1852 the sales particulars pointed out 'The Pleasure Grounds are very Ornamental, and interspersed with Walks beneath luxuriantly growing Beech and other timber, and comprise the American Garden containing Magnolias, Rhododendrons, Azaleas and other Flowering Shrubs in great luxuriance, of great height, growth and beauty.' The site of the garden, a long valley running north and south, is sheltered from the prevailing winds. This provided good frost drainage and permitted, in particular, very early-flowering shrubs such as magnolias.

William Hubbard's daughter Marion married Sir Edmund Loder, whose nearby estate of High Beeches contained another distinguished garden. The Loders became something of a horticultural dynasty, owning a third garden in the vicinity, Wakehurst Place, which is now the country department of Kew Gardens. Sir Edmund acquired the Leonardslee estate from his in-laws in 1889 and started a formidable programme of planting. It was he who bred the Loderi hybrid rhododendrons, the result of a cross between *R. griffithianum* and *R. fortunei*, all of which have white or pink deliciously scented flowers. Sir Edmund's grandson Sir Giles took over from him and continued to add to the plantings, taking a particular interest in camellias. His son Robin now runs the estate.

A series of seven lakes stretch through the bottom of the valley at Leonardslee. These were used in iron smelting to provide power for the furnace or for mechanical hammers. Today their banks are richly planted with ornamental trees such as swamp cypress (*Taxodium distichum*) and the Chinese redwood *Metasequioa glyptostroboides*; from time

to time the trees open out into glades by the water's edge. The slopes above are clothed in an exceptional collection of flowering shrubs with camellias, magnolias and rhododendrons given pride of place. Spring is clearly the most dazzling season from the point of view of flowers, but the autumn provides a scarcely less beautiful display, for there are countless deciduous trees – birches, maples, oaks, rowans, *Liquidambar styraciflua* and tupelos (*Nyssa sylvatica*) – which give brilliant colour. But the most memorable thing at Leonardslee (apart from the charming wallabies allowed to roam wild) is the combination of a beautiful and varied natural site with planting of exceptional beauty.

ABOVE *Rhododendrons press in on either side of the path with trees providing the shade that many of them need.*

FAR LEFT *The rock garden was made in about 1910 by Pulham & Co. The smaller rhododendrons and conifers are underplanted with ferns, Solomon's seal, primulas and Welsh poppies.*

Mapperton House

DORSET

It is the mixture of ingredients that fixes the gardens of Mapperton so firmly in the memory. The house evokes a rare display of emotion in Pevsner's *Buildings of England* volume on Dorset – 'There can hardly be anywhere', he writes, 'a more enchanting manorial group than Mapperton.' It is a beguiling mixture of periods, ranging from the 16th to the 18th centuries, all built in the lovely tawny stone of Ham Hill. Its setting is about as perfect as a house could have, at the head of a steep combe running southwards towards the sea. For hundreds of years the estate passed by inheritance, sometimes through the female

The lower pool is part of a much older formal garden. An avenue of clipped yews lines its sides with, at its far end, Elysian views down the combe where the land falls away abruptly.

line, until it was bought in 1919 by Mrs Labouchère. On her death in 1955 it was sold to Victor Montagu who disclaimed the titles of Viscount Hinchingbrooke and Earl of Sandwich to which he was heir.

All old houses have traces of past gardens but Mapperton is rather unusual in having very little evidence apart from what may be seen on the ground. The tithe map of 1841 shows a pattern of formal gardens in the

valley to the east of the house and the Ordnance Survey map of 1886 shows an avenue running along the drive and continuing into the field south of the house. But the major development in the garden took place in about 1927 when the estate was owned by Mrs Labouchère. She laid out in the valley an ambitious formal garden, of Italianate character, and very much in the tradition of the architects' gardens of the Arts and Crafts movement that had flourished before World War I. The site is a splendid one, rather hidden at first to the visitor, although handsomely displayed from the upper windows of the east front of the house.

There had plainly been formal gardens here before – the crisply formed turf slope on the west side is probably 17th century, the brick walls forming the garden boundary to the east are 18th century and the elegant little summerhouse built into the wall that separates the upper and lower gardens is 17th-century.

It seems almost certain that the designer of the new formal garden was a local architect, Charles Williams Pike. The garden, now called the Fountain Court, was disposed on a series of terraces, paved in stone, arranged in a cruciform pattern with a pool at the centre and a cross axis leading up steps on either side and linking two summerhouses built into the

An ornamental pavilion makes a visual link and joins the two levels of the formal pool and the sunken garden above it.

bank on one side and the wall on the other. It is ornamented with composition stone benches, lead figures, vases and topiary of strongly architectural character, often made of mixed box and yew. From the southern end of the Fountain Court the 17th-century summerhouse gives views of two long canal-like pools which continue the main axis of the garden down the valley. These, former fish ponds, have not been dated exactly but evidence of the reshaping of their boundaries

– which today are neatly linear – suggests that they may be quite ancient. Beyond the pools the valley garden continues in more informal vein, embellished with trees and shrubs planted by Victor Montagu. He, too, removed a 19th-century glasshouse at the north end of the Fountain Court and replaced it with a large orangery.

From the east front of the house the view is quintessentially English. Below, the intricate formal garden lies spread out, evidence of the old English love of classical order, but beyond it the unspoilt rural landscape testifies to the other, equally powerful, passion for nature.

Biddulph Grange

STAFFORDSHIRE

Most great gardens have similarities to others and are examples of a style that has common characteristics. Biddulph Grange, while being emphatically the product of its time, is unique. It dates entirely from the 19th century and was made by three people: James Bateman, his wife Maria and Edward Cooke. Bateman came from a prosperous family that had made its fortunes in the industrial revolution. As a child of eight he was shown a wild orchid by his mother – and orchids became 'the master passion of my life'. In his twenties he built up a remarkable collection of orchids at the family house of Knypersley Hall and between 1837 and 1843 published *Orchidaceae of Mexico and Guatemala*. In 1838 he married Maria Egerton-Warburton of a distinguished Cheshire family of great gardeners and in the early 1840s moved to a former vicarage at Biddulph, not far from Knypersley. In 1847 Bateman met Edward Cooke. An artist and discerning gardener, Cooke was also the son-in-law of George Loddiges whose nursery at Hackney was the greatest collection of commercially available plants in the world. Bateman and Cooke redesigned the house, turning it into a grandiose Italianate mansion, and started to lay out a garden on ground sloping to the south and east. Formal gardens near the house were the first to be built, with terraces and balustrades descending towards a lake. About the lake they planted rhododendrons which at this time mostly came from North America – this part of the garden used to be called the American Garden. To one side of the lake the Glen, a rocky ravine, was planted with ferns and rhododendrons. A curving tunnel led through to a pinetum which was planted with many of the newly introduced conifers of the day.

Victorian gardeners had a taste for the exotic which at Biddulph was given full rein in the parts of the garden known as China and Egypt. China was reached by passing through a dark tunnel from which the visitor suddenly emerged in a dazzling scarlet and gold Chinese temple overlooking a secluded pool, with an ornate bridge spanning a stream, the whole fringed with such oriental plants as *Acer palmatum* and *Cryptomeria japonica*. A picturesque fake Cheshire cottage backs onto, and forms an entrance to, Egypt – a stone temple containing a statue of the grotesque Ape of Thor, and guarded by a pair of sphinxes flanked by monumental yew topiary clipped into giant obelisks.

In front of the house a stepped path led between beds of dahlias backed by yew hedges. This, with rich colours against the sombre green of the yew, must have been inspired by the famous yew-hedged herbaceous borders made at Arley Hall by Maria Bateman's brother.

Biddulph was sold in 1871 and the house destroyed by fire in 1896. It was rebuilt and became a hospital in 1923. It then entered a period of decline and suffered appallingly from vandalism. It was acquired by the National Trust in 1988 and has since been magnificently restored so that every feature described above is in a better state than it can have been at any time since the Batemans lived, and may be relished by visitors.

The restored Italian Garden in spring – ramparts of rhododendrons flank a path leading down to the lake. The narrow borders on either side of the path have rows of Irish junipers underplanted with annuals.

Warwick Castle

hen German garden connoisseur and traveller Prince Pückler-Muskau visited Warwick Castle in 1826 he was overwhelmed by the history of the place and its beautiful setting – 'It was an enchanted spot, enveloped in the most charming robe of poetry, surrounded with all the majesty of history, the sight of which still fills me with delightful astonishment.' The castle, rising on a bluff above the river Avon, was started in the 11th century. Henry de Beaumont, one of William the Conqueror's followers, was put in charge of it and was later created 1st Earl of Warwick. The earldom of Warwick

has since passed through several families but the association with the castle continued until it was sold to the Tussauds Group by the 8th Earl (of the Greville family) in 1978.

Gardens are mentioned at Warwick Castle in the 16th century – 'the queen's gardens next Avon without the castle wall', which ran along the river west of the castle. In 1634 it was visited by Lieutenant Hammond, who records 'delightfull and shady walkes, and Arbors, pleasant Groves, and wildernesses, Fruitful trees, delicious Bowers, odiferous Herbes'. A map of 1711 shows a pattern of formal gardens on the same site as the

ABOVE *The Peacock Garden in front of the 18th-century conservatory was laid out in 1869 by Robert Marnock. The planting is modern but it preserves an appropriately lively Victorian flavour.*

Elizabethan garden and a parterre to the north-east. By the end of the 18th century all this had gone to be superseded by Capability Brown's landscaping. Brown was first called in by Francis Greville, Lord Brooke, in 1749, very early in his career when he was hardly known. He removed the formal gardens and gave the castle the appearance of rising from trees and meadows, and on the periphery of the castle park he planted belts and clumps of trees. Horace Walpole visited in 1751 shortly after Brown's work had taken effect – 'The castle is enchanting; the view pleased me more than I can express; the river Avon tumbles down a cascade at the foot of it. It is well laid out by one Brown.'

Later in the 18th century, under George Greville, a conservatory was built to house the famous Warwick Vase, which had been discovered in fragments at Hadrian's Villa in 1770-71. The conservatory, with elaborate Gothic tracery panes in arched windows, was completed in 1778 and the castle accounts refer to '969 feet of Best Bristol Glass in the sashes'.

In the 19th century there were two important additions to the gardens. In 1869 Robert Marnock, the influential curator of the Royal Botanic Society's garden in Regent's Park, designed a hexagonal flower parterre – now called the Peacock Garden – in front of the conservatory. In the same year he laid out a formal rose garden whose original designs were rediscovered by Paul Edwards in the County Record Office. This has been triumphantly reinstated, with arbours festooned with rambling roses, using old varieties and the new pink perpetual-flowering rose 'Warwick Castle', specially bred by David Austin.

The view from the Peacock Garden, framed by beautiful cedars of Lebanon, still shows the Avon curving peacefully in Brown's landscape. But this Grade I listed landscape has survived only by the skin of its teeth – an application to build a golf course on Brown's park was rejected in 1992 only as the result of the most skilful and energetic lobbying.

LEFT *The castle seen perched on its hill above the river Avon.*

117

Melbourne Hall

DERBYSHIRE

The importance of the garden at Melbourne Hall is that it is the only surviving work of the royal gardener to Queen Anne, Henry Wise; his other grand schemes, at some of the greatest estates of the day such as Longleat and Chatsworth, were obliterated by the subsequent craze for a more naturalistic landscaped garden. The garden at Melbourne – a formal pattern of long vistas – was commissioned in 1704 by Sir Thomas Coke whose desire was, in a famous quotation, to have a new garden 'to suit with Versailles'.

The family had come to Melbourne in 1628 when Sir John Coke was Secretary of State to King Charles I. The house he bought was chiefly 16th century but its appearance today is almost entirely 18th century in character. Sir John's grandson, Thomas, inherited in 1692 and plunged immediately into his garden schemes, ordering plants from the Brompton Nursery in which Henry Wise was a partner. Although the garden that Wise laid out was thought to be in the French style it was, in fact, eccentrically English. To start with, it is on quite a modest scale, just 10 acres – a great French formal garden was conceived on a grandiose scale and designed to seem to be without limits. Furthermore the chief pattern of walks hedged with clipped lime bears no visual relation to the house whereas a French garden in the style of Versailles would always be related axially to the house. At Versailles itself the palace is centred on an east-west axis – a deliberate reference to the Sun King – and all parts of

ABOVE *A figure of Mercury ornaments the view from the east front of the house. Its origins are not known but it is a version of one of the best-known works of the 16th-century Italian sculptor Giambologna.*

OPPOSITE *The setting sun gilds Robert Bakewell's wrought-iron birdcage arbour which seems to float in the pool that spreads out before it.*

the garden relate to it. The garden historian David Green wrote of Melbourne that it is 'the perfect compromise, the formal garden grown informal and English: the bob-tailed sheep-dog that was at first taken to be a poodle'.

Wise's layout was embellished with marvellous ornaments. Among them are many statues by John Van Nost, the foremost garden sculptor of the time, who made the huge Four Seasons Vase presented by Queen Anne to Sir Thomas Coke when he was her Vice Chamberlain. A bill for it for £100 survives dated 1706 – a huge sum in comparison, say, to the £42 which was paid for the '4 pr of Boyes cast in metall', the charming amorini which are still to be seen at Melbourne. Dating from the same period of Van Nost's activities is an exquisite wrought-iron arbour in the form of a domed birdcage made by the local blacksmith, Robert Bakewell. The Duchess of Chandos, visiting in 1706, described it as 'the most extra-ordinary observed in ye garden – an Arbour or Summer House made of very neat ironwork'. It was carefully positioned to make a visual link between the vista from the east front of the house and the Four Seasons vase which sits on an eminence where the *allées* of the formal garden meet.

The essential layout of the early 18th-century garden at Melbourne, and much of its detail, survive in a remarkably un-changed state. There remain to this day the original lime hedges, a superb tunnel of yew between whose gnarled trunks visitors may walk, Bakewell's wrought ironwork and Van Nost's lead statues placed at strategic points and much else. There have, of course, been additions and alterations – including some excellent modern planting – but what gives Melbourne its special charm is Henry Wise's 'bob-tailed sheep-dog' of a garden.

Oxford Botanic Garden

OXFORDSHIRE

The first botanic gardens of which we have detailed knowledge were made in Europe in the 16th century as part of the explosion of scientific enquiry that was associated with the Renaissance. In England the Renaissance took longer to have its effect and the first botanic garden was founded at Oxford, in 1621, planted with 'diverse simples for the advancement of the faculty of medicine'. These gardens, often called 'Physic Gardens', had two roles: first, as 'a repository of curious plants' to be studied scientifically as natural phenomena; and second, to investigate their use in medicine.

The site for the new garden, which it still occupies, was in the High Street by the banks of the river Cherwell. To raise the garden a little to prevent flooding there was added '4,000 loads of mucke and dunge laid by H. Windiatt the Universities scavenger'. Nicholas Stone, a master mason associated with Inigo Jones, was commissioned to make ornamental gateways which were built between 1632 and 1633 – they still survive and the main entrance, on the High Street, is one of the most splendid of all garden gateways. John Evelyn

saw the garden in 1653 – 'where the sensitive plant was shew'd us for a greate wonder'. This was the tropical *Mimosa pudica*, then quite recently introduced, whose leaves fold up when touched. But this was early in the garden's history and Evelyn notes: 'There grew canes, olive-trees, rhubarb, but no extraordinary curiosities, besides very good fruit which when the ladies had tasted we returned…to our lodgings'.

An engraved plan of the Oxford *Hortus Botanicus* by Loggan, dated 1675, shows a symmetrical four-part layout divided by a cruciform pattern of paths, with each of the four chief beds subdivided into four smaller ones. Some of these are arranged in decorative maze-like designs but others are disposed in plain rectangular 'order' beds in which plants were grouped according to their botanical characteristics. Exactly similar beds may be seen in the garden today. Loggan's print shows clearly that the garden was not planned for scientific purposes alone, for it is ornamented with topiary and each of the four paths has its eye-catcher. Just inside the main gate was a pair of topiary guardsmen pun-

ningly referred to at the time as 'the yewmen of the guard'. Celia Fiennes visited the garden in 1699 and wrote: 'The Physick Garden afforded great diversion and pleasure, the variety of flowers and plants would have entertained one a week'.

Under a series of distinguished keepers the fame of the garden was established. In 1721 the keeper was John Jacob Dillenius who received a visit from the great Linnaeus of whom he was extremely suspicious, referring to him as 'the man who has thrown all botany into confusion'. Later, walking in the garden, they paused to discuss a plant of ivy-leafed toadflax (*Cymbalaria muralis*) found growing in a wall. Linnaeus, according to the Oxford historian Mavis Batey, 'gave such a masterly analysis of the plant…that Dillenius was exceedingly impressed and offered to share his house and salary with him if he would stay in Oxford as his assistant'.

The garden continues as an important botanical research centre but it is also of interest to non-botanists. A wide range of well-grown ornamental plants flourishes here and its walled seclusion gives it irresistible charm.

OPPOSITE *Bougainvillea climbs on* Trachycarpus fortunei *in the glasshouse.*

LEFT *Water lilies and reeds flourish in the glasshouse.*

Athelhampton House

DORSET

In the sunken garden, 12 giant pyramids of clipped yew surround a central fountain. On one side, a terraced walk gives elevated views over the formal garden.

In the sunken garden, 12 giant pyramids of clipped yew surround a central fountain. On one side, a terraced walk gives elevated views over the formal garden.

In the 19th century English garden designers, for the first time, became keenly interested in the garden styles of the past and many of their designs were strongly influenced by studying historic garden layouts. The culmination of this tradition was the school of 'architectural' garden designers whose best work was carried out on either side of the turn of the century. Athelhampton (1891-99), designed by Francis Inigo Thomas, is one of the finest examples of the new garden in the old manner.

At Athelhampton Thomas found a marvellous old stone house possessing the vivid character of vernacular architecture that was so appreciated. It was built in the 15th century for Sir William Martyn who was Lord Mayor of London in 1493 and remained in the family until divided in 1590. It then suf-

fered from a series of changes of ownership and use until 1891 when, in a state of dereliction, it was bought and restored by Alfred Cart de Lafontaine who commissioned Thomas to design a new garden. Thomas, in collaboration with Sir Reginald Blomfield, was the author of *The Formal Garden in England* (1892) which had a great influence on garden design. The book had two purposes: the first was to assert the importance of a unity between house and garden – the garden should reflect the architectural principles that govern the design of the house; the second was to attack the garden philosophy of William Robinson who believed in 'copying nature's graceful touch'.

The garden that Thomas made may be seen by visitors today almost exactly as the architect designed it. It consists in essence of

four interconnected enclosures, the first of which spreads out below the gabled south façade of the house. At the centre of this rectangular space, which is on the axis of the garden door, a long pool 'catches the reflection of the house' as Thomas intended. From the centre of the pool a cross vista links the two other enclosures. The first is the dazzling circular Corona Garden with walls that dip in

a series of concave sweeps that rise to finials of stone obelisks. The whole is backed by yew hedges and water splashes in a central fountain. Steps lead from the Corona to the sunken garden where 12 giant pyramids of clipped yew are disposed about a central pool and fountain. The pyramids, over 100 years old, are now well over 10 metres high and their annual clipping is a major project. On the far side of the sunken garden a raised terrace, with an elegant pavilion at each end, allows sweeping views of the formal gardens.

Robert Victor Cooke came to live at Athelhampton in 1957 and did much to restore the gardens and added some excellent new planting. His grandson now lives there and the gardens are very well maintained. They still have the atmosphere evoked in the *Country Life* article of 1899 describing them in their recently completed state: 'Down in the water-meadows some miles out of Dorchester the clustered gables and battlements of Athelhampton nestle under the spreading boughs of a great cedar, and in the secluded courts can be heard the gentle coo of pigeons and the conversational patter of falling water.'

Renishaw Hall

'He walks up and down, surveying his work, which will never be finished, his head full of new projects of sun and shade, but never of flowers, measuring the various views with a stick to his eye or a pair of binoculars.' In these words Sir Osbert Sitwell in his autobiography, *Left Hand, Right Hand*, described his father Sir George Sitwell's passion for gardening. Sir George was, in a notably extreme form, the archetype of the English gardener overwhelmed by a love for the gardens of the Italian Renaissance. From the 16th century onwards English travellers had found their way to Italy, and among the sights that fixed themselves most emphatically in their memories were the great gardens of the Renaissance. From the 1890s onwards Sir George visited over 200 Italian gardens, studied them intimately and distilled their essence in his mind. The qualities that most struck him were the relationship of the garden with its surroundings, the value of water and the importance of surprise. Sir George wrote a book summing up these ideas, *An Essay on the Making of Gardens* (1909), whose subtitle was 'A Study of Old Italian Gardens, of the Nature of Beauty, and the Principles involved in Garden Design'. With these principles in mind he set about transforming his own garden at Renishaw.

The Sitwell family has lived in or near Renishaw since the 14th century and in 1625 built the first Renishaw Hall whose present appearance is almost entirely due to the first baronet, Sir Sitwell Sitwell, who completely rebuilt it between 1793 and 1808. He removed nearly all traces of earlier pleasure gardens and when Sir George inherited the estate in 1887 there was little of horticultural interest left. The new, Italianate, garden that he made survives almost entirely intact today. It is disposed about a central axis on gently sloping land aligned with the chief entrance in the south façade of the house. A series of terraces linked by stone steps descends in stately progression. Each terrace is enlivened with yew topiary clipped into abstract shapes – pyramids with square tops, and domed columns. Sir George imported excellent statues from Italy which stand on pedestals on either side of the stone steps. In the centre of the lowest terrace a circular pool with a single jet of water is flanked by monumental

RIGHT *To one side of the terraced garden, statues of a warrior and an Amazon flank the entrance to a woodland walk of hollies. Their pedestals are festooned with boldly variegated ivy.*

OPPOSITE *Steps linking different levels of the terraced garden are decorated with triumphant Italian statues on raised plinths. The planting of shrub roses and vines softens the crisp architectural detail.*

pyramids of yew. Sir George was uninterested in flowers and considered 'such flowers as might be permitted…(should not) call attention to themselves by hue or scent'. Although he consulted Gertrude Jekyll, who submitted planting schemes, her advice was not taken.

The lowest terrace has views overlooking the Rother Valley, with the great Cavendish

A cross vista in the terraced garden shows contrasting shapes of urns and topiary. Hedges of sombre yew are enlivened with the sort of ornamental planting of which Sir George Sitwell strongly disapproved.

house of Bolsover sometimes visible in the distance. As Sir George wrote: 'The garden must be considered not as a thing in itself, but as a gallery of foregrounds designed to set off the soft hues of the distance.' The garden at Renishaw, firmly based on theory, provides a distinguished setting for the house and a memorable proscenium for views of the landscape beyond the garden.

Packwood House

Packwood House was built by the Fetherston family in the late 16th century. The estate was passed down the family, once through the female line, until the late 19th century. In 1905 it was sold at auction to Alfred Ash who had made a fortune in metal in Birmingham – his obituary in 1925 recorded that 'he viewed life from the sunny side – and from the interior of a gorgeous Rolls-Royce'. His son Graham did much to restore the house and gave it to the National Trust in 1941.

A drawing of the house dated 1756 also shows some detail of the garden. The house is seen from the south with lavish half-timbering, gables and central chimney stack – a more modest affair than it is today, having been much extended by Graham Ash. The south forecourt is shown with its brick walls and a summerhouse built into the north-west corner. The garden within the walls has a sparse scattering of topiary, with larger specimens shaped into spirals. In the centre of the southern wall are gate piers and steps leading down, a series of brick semi-circles.

During the late 19th-century craze for architectural gardens and for topiary, Packwood was suddenly brought to public notice when Sir Reginald Blomfield, the great protagonist of the architectural garden, described it in his book *The Formal Garden in England* (1892). The walled south garden forecourt was much to his taste but it was the monumental yew garden beyond the garden wall that especially inspired him. 'Here,' he wrote, 'the Sermon on the Mount is literally represented in clipped yew. At the entrance to the "mount", at the end of the garden, stand four tall yews 20 ft high for the four evangelists and six on either side for the twelve apostles.' It was believed at the time that this was a surviving 17th-century symbolic garden – in fact most of the yews had been planted in the mid 19th century.

Whatever its origin, the Sermon on the Mount may be seen today in marvellous maturity. From the south forecourt the eye is drawn past the beautiful wrought-iron 18th-century gates along a dramatic procession of yews leading towards the mount. Graham Ash added a sunken garden in the forecourt with a little pool and introduced low hedges of yew. In recent times the borders in this part of the garden have been revitalised and are now densely planted in brilliantly colourful schemes, forming a cheerful prelude to the more solemn pleasures of the yew topiary beyond the wall. These borders are entirely herbaceous and some are rather narrow, needing meticulous staking to keep the plants in immaculate order.

Looking down from the south façade of the house in high summer the visitor sees a charming and remarkably eclectic vision. The crisp 18th-century enclosure, with its Arts and Crafts touches of the early 20th century, is blurred by the dazzling, essentially late 20th-century planting, and beyond it the great parade of topiary stands to attention. This mixture of garden styles, with each period being given its due weight, and the refusal to preserve a garden as an unchanging monument to the past, present an exhilarating spectacle.

Columns of solemn yew rise above the terrace walk with its brilliant borders lavishly planted in exuberant Victorian style.

Saling Hall

The life of a garden is relatively short and always dependent on the continuing interest and imagination of the owner. Saling Hall is a seductive late Elizabethan house built of lovely Essex brick, decorated a hundred years later with those curvaceous Dutch-style gables that give so many East Anglian houses their specially attractive character. Pretty as the house is, and not discounting the activities of earlier gardeners here, it is under the present ownership that the place has developed its true garden distinction.

Historically the exceptional garden feature of Saling Hall is the walled garden that spreads out west of the house. Very unusually, its walls bear a date – 1698 – and were added when the house was enlarged by Martin Carter. This enclosure, with its fine brick walls, has the rural, unsophisticated formality that such a garden might have had in the early 18th century. Borders line the walls and paths of brick laid in herringbone pattern run down the middle and along the borders on either side. The ornamental planting is mostly due to the present owner, Hugh Johnson, but he preserved some lively and idiosyncratic features that contribute powerfully to its character – flanking rows of ancient pollarded apple trees, a procession of columnar Lawson cypresses (*Chamaecyparis lawsoniana* 'Pottenii') leading down the borders on either side and echoing rows of Irish juniper (*Juniperus communis* 'Hibernica') that run down the borders on either side of the central path. This mature structural planting gives harmony to the richly planted borders.

In the walled garden Hugh Johnson has fine-tuned an existing layout. But in the woodland to the north of the house his love of trees, and taste for landscaping, have been given full rein. When he came here over 20 years ago this area was chiefly elms and poplars, which provided a welcome windbreak against the coldest winds. This is generally flat country but the woodland here has a subtle rise and fall. Disease despatched the splendid elms and, as choicer plantings of trees – some very rare – have been added, the poplars have been all but eliminated. Furthermore, glades and vistas have been opened up, providing visual links and ornamental interludes among the trees. A sketch of a Japanese garden has box clipped into mounds swirling down a bank and a little cascade tumbling into a pool. Another pool has a promontory with a group of Himalayan birches (*Betula* 'Jermyns') whose pale stems echo the Tuscan columns of an elegant temple on the far boundary. A long ride is enlivened by a giant stone ball mounted on a slight eminence as an eye-catcher. These effects are unobtrusive, giving a sense of repose without detracting from the main attraction – the very interesting and varied collection of trees which provide something worth looking at on any day of the year.

The area of the garden at Saling Hall is about 12 acres, including water garden and other ornamental plantings closer to the house. By modern standards this is large, but such is the range of visual effects and the richness of the planting, that it seems even larger.

LEFT *In the arboretum, clearings are ornamented with statues. A figure of Bacchus is especially appropriate, for the garden belongs to the world's leading wine writer. Decorative features of this kind complement the rich collection of trees.*

RIGHT *In the walled garden richly decorative planting is given structure by clipped pyramids of box and stately columns of Irish juniper (*Juniperus communis* 'Hibernica'). A mass of Alstroemeria 'Ligtu Hybrids' enlivens the foreground and a handsome lead figure of Flora stands among the foliage.*

Hackfall Wood

An interest in landscape, as an object of contemplation, was one of the essentials of 18th-century taste. Landscape became a suitable subject for painting and poetry and, for gardeners, a vital aspect of their art. The site of a garden, and its prospects, were all important. At Hackfall in North Yorkshire the rocky, wooded cliff plummeting 90 metres down to the river Ure was a site rich in possibilities. The estate had been bought by John Aislabie of Studley Royal but it was only after his death in 1741 that his son William started work on it. From about 1749 he made a garden that was the embodiment of the 18th-century idea of the sublime which Horace Walpole described as 'Precipices, mountains, torrents, wolves, rumblings, Salvator Rosa!'

After its completion Hackfall's fame spread fast. One of its essential buildings was a banqueting hall, built on a promontory, from whose windows the dramatic valley scenery was suddenly apparent to the visitor for the first time. In 1772 it was visited by the landscape connoisseur William Gilpin who wrote: 'You have not the least intimation of a design upon you; nor any suggestion that you are on high grounds; till the folding doors of the building at Mowbray-point being thrown open, you are struck with one of the grandest, and the most beautiful bursts of country that the imagination can form... Your eye is first carried many fathoms precipitately down a bold woody sweep, to the river Ewer...two promontories shoot into the river, in contrast to each other: that on the right is woody, faced with rock, and crowned with a castle: that on the left, rises smooth from the water, and is scattered with a few clumps...The foreground is as pleasing as the background.'

The visitor today may share Gilpin's

experience. Although the buildings have decayed, trees have been felled for timber and paths become obscured by bracken and brambles, Hackfall still gives the thrill of a plunge into the sublime. The approach is a path skirting a field and, as Gilpin said, 'you have not the least intimation of a design upon you'. You suddenly come upon the very brow of a cliff with on one side the distant eye-catcher of Mowbray Castle, built as a ruin in full Gothick castellated style, rising above the woods. Paths snake down through the woods leading to the gushing waters of the river Ure. The woods today are almost entirely self-sewn saplings and often the path is choked with undergrowth through which loom the ruins of a Gothick temple, Fisher's Hall. Eventually the visitor is rewarded by the

ABOVE *At the foot of the wooded slopes the curving river Ure is glimpsed from many parts of the garden.*

OPPOSITE *William Aislabie channelled swift-flowing streams through picturesque gulleys fringed with mossy rocks and ferns.*

sight of sparkling water and from the banks of the river Mowbray Castle is visible crowning the wooded heights above.

Until World War II Hackfall remained a famous beauty spot but was then forgotten until local enthusiasts took an interest in it. Today it belongs to the Woodland Trust and it is accessible all day and every day throughout the year. Although dishevelled, it still possesses the rare character that so impressed William Gilpin.

Misarden Park

*I*n old gardens an ancient framework often dictates the layout long after any original planting has disappeared. At Misarden Park the site is exceptionally beautiful and must always have had a powerful influence on the garden. It is a country of steep, wooded valleys and the house, on an elevated site well over 180 metres high, commands exquisite views over the Golden valley to the south. It was built in about 1616 for Sir William Sandys whose memorial may be seen in the village church. The estate remained in the Sandys family until 1839 since when it has changed hands several times. The house was remodelled by Alfred Waterhouse in 1875 and, after a fire in 1919, Sir Edwin Lutyens rebuilt the east wing, adding an elegant loggia.

Kip's engraving of Misarden Park in Atkyns' *Present and Ancient State of Glostershire* (1712) shows a pattern of formal gardens spreading out to the south and west of the house in very much the position of the formal gardens today. The planting of the gardens is almost entirely 20th century but these south-east-facing slopes, with their splendid views of the valley below, must always have seemed the obvious site for a garden. The present ensemble of enclosures and the formality softened by generous planting, is characteristic of a 20th-century layout. To the west of the house steps lead through fine wrought-iron gates to a virtuoso walk of clipped yew hedges that forms a firm axis for the ornamental schemes that lie to either side. The tops of the hedges have been clipped

132

into bold humps, like the crenellations of a giant castle, and the far end is marked by a stone urn. On one side of the yew walk a path passes under a tunnel of espaliered pears to a kitchen garden and formal rose garden. On the other side of the walk a pair of herbaceous borders runs the whole length of the hedge.

Closer to the house many of the details of the garden show signs of the Arts and Crafts movement which had great influence in Gloucestershire. Whether this comes from Lutyens' work here in 1920, or was merely the influence of the times, is not known. The little grey and silver garden above terraced drystone walls to the south-west of the house is a characteristic example. Here the mounds of santolina and artemisia and spreading waves of *Stachys byzantina* have distinct echoes of Gertrude Jekyll. The paved terrace running along the south façade of the house is edged with ramparts of yew topiary. If Lutyens himself did not recommend this it was certainly made by someone sympathetic to his ideas.

On the slopes below the house the gardens become much less formal as they merge with the encroaching country. Here are some distinguished trees – a handsome *Davidia involucrata*, and several trees with especially good autumn colour such as *Liquidambar styraciflua* and the graceful Katsura (*Cercidiphyllum japonicum*) whose branches have an elegant downward sweep. From the far corner of this little arboretum is a distant view of the Elizabethan stone manor house firmly rooted in its setting.

LEFT *Topiary ramparts of yew mark the edge of the south terrace below which are waves of the white willow herb* (Epilobium angustifolium album) *– lovely but dreadfully invasive.*

FAR LEFT *Steps lead up from the house through a fine gateway to the yew walk with its dramatically shaped hedges. A pale stone urn provides the perfect eye-catcher.*

Hatfield House

HERTFORDSHIRE

When John Evelyn visited Hatfield House in 1643, just over 30 years after it was built, he recorded in his diary that 'the most considerable rarity besides the house (inferior to few for its Architecture then in England) was the Garden & Vineyard rarely well water'd and planted'. Hatfield has the most fascinating garden history of almost any house in England. The house was begun in 1607 by Robert Cecil, the 1st Marquess of Salisbury, and very shortly afterwards he recruited as head gardener John Tradescant the Elder, who later became gardener to King Charles I. The John Tradescants, father and son, were central figures in 17th-century garden history, in touch with plant collectors internationally. The Hatfield archives record the flood of plants that came to the garden at this time – in 1611, 500 fruit trees from the French queen (Anne of Austria, wife to King Louis XIII); in 1612, 453 cherry trees and 1,200 limes sent from France at a cost of £140; and so on in bewildering quantity. Another key figure in the early history of the garden is the Frenchman Salomon de Caus, an extraordinary and mysterious figure who floated through the great houses of Europe creating fantastic grottoes and elaborate ornamental waterworks. The garden he made for the Elector Palatine Frederick V at Heidelberg – the legendary Hortus Palatinus – was one of the wonders of the day. At Hatfield from 1611 onwards he made the 'Great Water Parterre', a formal lake with an island and banqueting house.

A painting of the house and gardens from about 1740, surviving at Hatfield, shows the walls and divisions of the magnificent formal gardens of the previous century, but now choked with trees. Later in the 18th century these walls were swept away and parkland, in the fashion of the day, went up to the very walls of the house. By the time the encyclopedist J. C. Loudon visited in 1825 he recorded that 'the gardens afford little to gratify the amateur'. In the 1840s the Marquess of Salisbury, in anticipation of a royal visit from Queen Victoria, rebuilt walls and terraces and reinstated much of the formal character of the Jacobean gardens.

Since 1972 the gardens at Hatfield have been transformed again by the present Marchioness of Salisbury, who had already reinvigorated another Cecil garden, at Cranborne Manor in Dorset. At Hatfield she preserved the best of the past but has added and improved throughout the garden. Underneath the walls of the Old Palace – where Queen Elizabeth I was confined as a girl during her sister Mary's reign – she laid out a knot garden with box-edged divisions enclosing collections of historic plants from different periods, including one of 17th-century plants honouring the Tradescant connection. In the Privy Garden she retained the Victorian yew hedges and planted exuberant mixed borders rich in roses and peonies. The East Gardens, the site of much of the Marquess of Salisbury's work in the 1840s, has been transformed, keeping some of the earlier pattern but adding on either side walks of clipped holm oaks (*Quercus ilex*), Italian statues and lively new planting in the borders. In her interest in historic gardening styles, and great knowledge of garden plants, Lady Salisbury is a characteristic late 20th-century gardener. In one further respect she is also very much in tune with the times. The gardens at Hatfield are maintained entirely organically, no pesticides or herbicides being allowed.

LEFT *A new entrance courtyard was made in the 1840s as part of the comprehensive restoration of the gardens in honour of Queen Victoria's visit in 1846.*

OPPOSITE *Under the walls of the Old Palace, which predates the present house by more than a hundred years, the Marchioness of Salisbury has laid out a patchwork of period gardens. In the foreground is a simple maze and behind it are collections of historic garden plants of different periods. A terraced walk, in Tudor style, overlooks this part of the garden.*

Levens Hall

The garden at Levens Hall is a remarkably complete survival of a provincial formal layout from the end of the 17th century. It was made by Colonel James Grahme, former Privy Purse to King James II, who bought – or won at gaming if one believes the more romantic account – this ancient Cumbrian estate in 1688. The designer of his new garden was the Frenchman Guillaume Beaumont whose portrait painted in about 1700 survives at the house, inscribed 'Monsieur Beaumont Gardener to King James 2nd & to Col. Jas. Grahme. He laid out the Gardens at Hampton Court Palace and at Levens.' Although Beaumont worked on other gardens in England, notably Nunningham, Longleat and Forde Abbey, nothing of his work remains except at Levens. It is probable that, well-versed in the techniques of André le Nôtre, he was one of those skilled French gardeners who came to England with the restored King Charles II. However, it should also be said that the garden he made at Levens is strikingly unlike anything made in France.

A water-colour plan – 'A Map of Leavens garding' – of c.1730 by Robert Skyring, on display in the house, shows a pattern of formal gardens extending north and west from the house whose detail corresponds remarkably with the layout of the whole garden today. The most striking difference in this layout from fashionable French schemes of the period is the lack of any dominating axis linking different parts of the garden to the house. Levens Hall garden became well-known quite early on and eager visitors sought permission from Monsieur Beaumont – who lived on the estate – to inspect it. A

Immediately to the west of the house a pattern of beds edged in box is filled with topiary shapes – 'a peacock here, a huge umbrella-like construction there, an archway, a lion…and a host of other such adornments all shaped out of ductile yew' as *Country Life*

1730 plan, beyond which a ha-ha, quite possibly the oldest in England, separates the garden from the parkland beyond.

All this could so easily have become a desiccated museum-garden but few ancient gardens give the appearance of being so full of

OPPOSITE *In autumn the freshly clipped yew topiary presents sharp outlines above beds filled with the wormwood* Artemisia *'Powis Castle'.*

LEFT *Much of the yew topiary has assumed an attractive irregularity giving the appearance of great age.*

letter addressed to 'Mr Beaumont att Leavens' reads: 'Sr the bearers hereof being part of my family hath a desire to see the Garden at leavenss if it may be a proper time to admitt them & their acquaintance it will be taken as a great favour & will much oblige Sr your humble servtt Robt Hubbersley.' Visitors continued throughout the garden's history; today they are more numerous than ever and can see the garden as beautifully maintained as it can ever have been.

rather pompously put it in 1899. Some of this topiary may well be original but much is certainly far more recent; early Victorian views, such as the engraving in Joseph Nash's *Mansions of England in Olden Times* (1847), show striking differences from the modern shapes. South of the house, however, the great beech alley, with its central rondel, is an extraordinary survival from the original layout. A cross axis from the rondel leads westwards to a bastion, also visible on the

life as Levens is today. The topiary garden is beautifully cared for and enlivened with well-judged annual plantings. Good new borders have been made in appropriate places and a splendid new fountain was created to celebrate the tercentenary of the garden in 1994. All this has been achieved by the private funds and energies of the present owners to whom the estate has ultimately descended by inheritance from Colonel Grahme.

Stourhead

WILTSHIRE

This is the most famous and most visited landscape garden in England. Like many other gardens of great originality it represents the vision not of some professional designer but of a single highly cultivated amateur. It was created by Henry Hoare whose family, originally goldsmiths in London, had turned to banking in the 17th century. Henry Hoare's father, another Henry, had acquired the Stourton estate in 1717 and commissioned from Colen Campbell an exquisite Palladian mansion which was completed in about 1724.

In the 1740s Henry Hoare II started to lay out his garden on a site at some distance from the house, indeed invisible from it, on the banks of the river Stour. He created a roughly triangular lake by damming the river and began to embellish its shores with buildings designed by the architect Henry Flitcroft. Among these early buildings are the Temple of Flora, the Grotto and the Pantheon and it seems to have been Hoare's intention from the start to compose his garden in such a way as to resemble a series of exquisitely framed views. Unlike the slightly earlier Rousham House, which directed attention to Arcadian scenes outside the garden, Stourhead is enclosed and inward looking. Hoare made a circuit path girdling the lake which presents perpetually shifting views of the buildings – across water, half-veiled by trees or rising on an eminence above the path.

The Grotto was planned as an abrupt change of mood. It lies on the circuit path from which the visitor would descend, at one moment walking in the sun and the next plunged into the shivery gloom of a subterranean cavern. The antiquary John Britton, writing in 1801, perfectly caught its atmosphere: 'It will be impossible for me to describe the awful sensations which I experienced on entering its gloomy cells; my fancy was set afloat on an ocean of conjecture...Its seclusion among woods, contiguity to the waters, subterranean approach, rattling cascades, marble basins and silent statues.' The Grotto is embellished by the figure of a river god, the deity of the river Stour, holding an urn from which the river flows. To one side an opening in the rock-work frames serene views of the Temple of Flora on the other side of the lake. It is these composed views, so close in spirit to the paintings of Claude, that for many visitors will be the most unforgettable memory of Stourhead.

There have been attempts to explain the whole layout of the gardens and its sequence of buildings in terms of the journeys of Aeneas and the founding of Rome as described in Virgil's *Aeneid*. There are Virgilian references – the Temple of Flora is inscribed with the famous words from the *Aeneid: Procul, o procul este profani* – 'Be gone, be gone you who are not believers' – but no-one has made a convincing explanation of the garden in these terms. The abundance of classical references, which would have delighted Henry Hoare's cultivated Grand Tourist friends, may go unrecognised by most modern visitors, but the garden's power of enchantment is as effective today as it was then.

The Palladian bridge spans a stream leading into the lake on whose far shore Henry Flitcroft's Pantheon rises on a grassy mound.

Iford Manor

*I*ford combines, at one splendid site, two distinctive English gardening themes – a love of the classical past and a taste for rural life. The house is a very attractive one – the stone facade, of classical inspiration, dates from the 1720s but the house's origins are much older. It lies on the wooded slopes of the Frome valley, right on the border between Somerset and Wiltshire, with the river flowing a few yards from the house. The estate was bought in 1899 by the architect Harold Peto who lived here until his death in 1933. Peto had been in partnership with Ernest George and their firm had built up one of the most flourishing country-house architectural practices of the late Victorian period. The partnership was dissolved in 1892 on the agreement that Peto would not compete with his former colleagues for business in this country. Henceforth most of his architectural work was done in the South of France, although he designed several gardens in England. In his work on Riviera villa gardens he was very strongly influenced by the ideas of the Italian Renaissance garden. His designs were strongly architectural with

ABOVE *The terraces are linked by a precipitous flight of stairs made, in true Arts and Crafts tradition, out of a mixture of drystone walling and beautifully cut limestone, with fine lead urns ornamenting the piers.*

boldly conceived vistas linking the different parts, and much disciplined use of ornaments and garden buildings. During his time in the South of France he made a collection of statuary, ornaments and architectural fragments of varied provenance which he was to use to good effect at Iford.

At Iford the site had the advantage of a steep slope rising above the house, although the views were limited by the steep valley. The garden behind the house had already been terraced before Peto arrived – probably in the 18th century – and there were picturesque winding walks in the hanging woods above the garden.

The terraced garden faces south-west and is divided into three parts. Immediately behind the house is an arcaded loggia from which steps lead up to two terraces with an oval lily pool, lawns and borders beyond. The broad top terrace sweeps right across the northern

extremity of the formal garden with woodland soaring above providing an emphatic background. Here, artfully disposed, are fine old columns and balustrades from Peto's collection with, at one end, a well-head and seat, and at the other a little octagonal summerhouse of the same date as the house. From this top terrace, looking south across the wooded valley, with cattle grazing in

meadows in the distance and a foreground alive with beautifully arranged fragments of the past, the visitor may experience the essence of the place – a harmonious combination of English rural setting and Italianate garden layout.

There is richly varied planting everywhere at Iford but it is the repeated architectural evergreens that have the most telling effect –

yew, juniper, Italian cypresses (*Cupressus sempervirens*) and the Mediterranean *Phillyrea latifolia*. Harold Peto wrote in his manuscript *Boke of Iford*: 'Old buildings or fragments of masonry carry one's mind back to the past in a way that a garden of flowers only cannot do. Gardens that are too stony are equally unsatisfactory; it is the combination of the two in just proportion that is most satisfying.'

ABOVE *The uppermost terrace looks east towards the early 18th-century octagonal summerhouse. On the left, one of Harold Peto's beloved Italian cypresses* (Cupressus sempervirens) *gives an authentic whiff of the Mediterranean.*

Compton Acres

DORSET

*T*he gardens at Compton Acres are very much of their time and they have been maintained in a wonderfully old-fashioned manner. They have an enviable site on the wooded slopes that lead to the cliffs that plummet down to the sea between Poole and Bournemouth. This part of the Dorset coast has much sunshine and the south-facing slopes and proximity to the sea give it a very mild micro-climate. The estate was bought in 1914 by Thomas William Simpson, a financier, when it was almost entirely rural. He decided to create a garden that consisted of a series of enclosed spaces of very different character linked together by paths winding down the slopes. In spirit, if not in execution, parts of the layout are close to the Arts and Crafts designers of the turn of the century and their 'architectural' gardens in which the paths, walls, masonry and ornaments were at least as important as the planting. Simpson died in 1950 by which time, because of shortage of labour during World War II, the gardens had

fallen into neglect. They were bought by an architect, J. S. Beard, who restored and added to them and they subsequently changed hands again, becoming not a private garden, but commercially run 'show gardens' presented as a tourist attraction.

The different parts of the gardens are either historical or stylistic – the Roman Garden, Italian Garden, Japanese Garden and so on – or based on a style of planting – the Woodland Walk, Tropical Dell, Rock Garden and Heather Dell. This kind of eclecticism has been a major theme in English garden history, although it is rare to see such a wide range of garden styles displayed in a single place. The Italian Garden, one of the first to which the visitor comes, has a long narrow lily pond with double stairs leading down at one end and a temple with a cupola at the other. Many urns and statues are arranged among borders that are planted out with bedding schemes. The Japanese Garden, at the end of the garden tour, was made by

Simpson after a visit to Kyoto. When Japan was opened to the West in the late 19th century, intense interest was aroused by Japanese culture. In music *The Mikado* (1885) and *Madame Butterfly* (1904) were immensely popular and there was a craze for Japanese gardens. At Compton Acres, Simpson chose a fine site and imported many items from Japan including the temple, tea house, stone lanterns and even trees.

The soil at Compton Acres is acid and the planting, with collections of azaleas, camellias, eucryphias, heathers, pieris and rhododendrons, takes full advantage of it. The mild microclimate and excellent drainage allows many tender plants. The visitor can find eucalyptus, the beautiful red-stemmed *Drimys lanceolata* from Chile, mimosas (*Acacia dealbata*) and pomegranates (*Punica granatum*). From the top of the hill, with the sea glinting below, and the immense range of plants spread out profusely, the place has much of the character of a Mediterranean garden.

RIGHT *The Italian Garden is unlike anything in Italy but, with its splashing water and brilliant bedding scheme, it has an appealing exuberance.*

OPPOSITE *The Japanese Garden was built after World War II with the help of Japanese gardeners. The ornaments and many of the plants were imported from Japan.*

Trebah

CORNWALL

RIGHT *Magnolias flower as early as February in the privileged environment of the ravine garden. Here the stately* Magnolia campbellii *rises above sheets of daffodils.*

The Fox family was one of those gardening dynasties that devised a distinctive Cornish type of garden. The shipping firm of G. C. Fox & Co. was founded at Falmouth in 1754 by the Quaker George Croker Fox whose family came to dominate horticultural life in the Falmouth area. In the mid 19th century three of their gardens were famous – Grove Hill, Rosehill and Penjerrick – and two other gardens earned their reputation a little later on – Glendurgan (now a property of the National Trust) and Trebah.

The site at Trebah, as with many of the great Cornish gardens, is the determining factor. It is a steep combe 600 metres long sloping southwards to the Helford river. The house at the head of the valley was built in about 1750 for the Nicholl family. Robert Were Fox of Rosehill gave the estate to his son Charles in 1842 who gardened assiduously until his death in 1868. The Fox estate of Glendurgan is immediately next door to Trebah, occupying a very similar site to the east, and when Charles Fox came to Trebah his cousin Alfred had already been developing Glendurgan, most notably planting in the 1820s immense windbreaks of maritime pine (*Pinus pinaster*) which gave vital protection to both gardens.

Charles Fox thinned the existing woodland and embarked on a programme of introducing rare exotics, obtaining some of the seed through his connections in the world of shipping. After his death the estate passed to his son-in-law Edmund Backhouse and eventually to another notable Cornish family, the Hexts who, right up until World War II, carried on the Fox tradition. There then followed a period of stagnation and neglect in which the fame of the garden was all but extinguished. In 1981 it was acquired by Major Hibbert who embarked on an ambitious programme of restoration and has set up a trust to ensure its survival. Today it is in a better state than for very many years.

The micro-climate is the *raison d'être* for the garden here coupled, perhaps, with the Quaker desire to make a perfect place in an imperfect world. The precipitous sides of the valley are laced with paths and the distinctive experience is of walking along these paths and admiring the shifting views across the valley and downwards over a bewildering profusion

LEFT *In the ravine garden, paths on either side give views over abundant exotic planting – ferns, a tree fern (*Dicksonia antarctica*) and tall Chusan palms (*Trachycarpus fortunei*).

of exotic planting. From the undergrowth, immensely tall Chusan palms (*Trachycarpus fortunei*) soar upwards and groves of tender tree ferns (*Dicksonia antarctica*), which are naturalised here, seem just as at home as in their native habitat of Tasmania. There are rhododendrons in profusion (some such as 'Trebah Gem' bred here) with pride of place certainly going to those large-leafed ever-green species such as *R. sinogrande* which nowhere in England will grow as they do in Cornwall. The great connoisseur of woody plants, W. J. Bean, described this as 'the most splendid and remarkable of all rhododen-drons, or indeed of all woody plants hardy in this country'. The greatest pleasure at Trebah is given by the sheer profusion of remarkable plants grown in such a dramatic setting.

Woburn Abbey

BEDFORDSHIRE

*T*he abbey at Woburn was a great Cistercian house, founded in 1145 by the monks of Fountains Abbey in Yorkshire. With the dissolution of the monasteries it passed in 1547 to John, Lord Russell, who later became the 1st Earl of Bedford. The Russells, apart from their great estate at Woburn, also owned property in London which they developed with great skill. In Covent Garden in the early 17th century and in Bloomsbury 150 years later they made a profound impact on the urban landscape.

The income from these estates allowed a continuing expenditure on the house and gardens at Woburn over a very long period of time during which some of the best architects and garden designers were employed. In the 1620s an exquisite Italianate Grotto room was commissioned and its design attributed to the architect and designer Isaac de Caus, a protégé of Inigo Jones, who worked in the 1630s on the replanning of Covent Garden for the 4th Earl. This enchanting room, vaulted and richly embellished with shell-work, survives in remarkable condition. It is not known how it was connected to the garden, nor indeed if it ever was, but it is certainly typical of the ornamental garden grottoes that were common in Europe in the 16th and 17th centuries. Later in the 17th century there was a formal garden, partly ornamental and partly planted with fruit and vegetables.

The 18th century saw the greatest garden activity at Woburn. Charles Bridgeman, the most important figure in the transition from formal to informal styles of gardening, was consulted in the 1720s. The 4th Duke of Bedford bought many exotic trees and shrubs from the sale of Lord Petre's great collection in 1746. From 1787 to 1802 the architect Henry Holland, Capability Brown's partner and son-in-law, did much work both on the house and on buildings in the estate. He built in the pleasure grounds a delightful polygonal

Chinese dairy with Chinoiserie furnishings. Apart from its great charm this garden building is important for two reasons. It is an exceptional example of an ornamental garden building with supposedly practical uses. Marie Antoinette's neo-classical dairy at Rambouillet, built in 1785, is perhaps the best known example of the tradition. The Woburn dairy is also evidence of fashionable English taste for Chinoiserie in the second half of the 18th century which saw its culmination in such buildings as Brighton Pavilion.

In the early 19th century the 6th Duke recruited Humphry Repton to carry out many improvements. Repton had already worked for the Duke's London estate, notably laying out the gardens of Russell Square in 1806. At

ABOVE *The base of this armillary sundial, in the private garden, is given a sympathetic fringe of deep blue* Lavandula angustifolia *'Hidcote'. The same lavender forms hedges for the rose beds behind.*

RIGHT *A brilliantly painted Chinese pagoda marks the centre of a circular maze of hornbeam* (Carpinus betulus). *In old mazes such centrepieces were often built so that instructions could be shouted from them to lost visitors.*

Woburn he was full of new ideas – for an ornamental menagerie (or 'animated garden' as he called it), a rose garden, a Chinese garden, alterations to the lake and a collection of American plants. He was able later to recollect that 'The Improvements I have had the honour to suggest have nowhere been so fully realized as at Woburn Abbey'.

Today, still owned by the Russell family, Woburn Abbey is one of the most visited great estates in England. Its best attractions for the modern garden visitor are the great park – a deer park in the middle ages – superb trees, and the various garden buildings from different periods that happily have survived.

Howick Hall

Close to the most beautiful part of the wild Northumbrian coast east of Alnwick, Howick Hall has a marvellous wooded, undulating site. The suave classical mansion, designed by William Newton of Newcastle, was built for Sir Henry Grey in 1782. Although so close to the sea, and some of the coldest winds in Britain, Howick enjoys the protection of a valley and some remarkably tender plants flourish here. Another curiosity of the site, which has also had a fundamental influence on the planting, is the unlikely juxtaposition of acid and alkaline soil. This is essentially limestone country but an area of about four acres, one quarter of the total, is a seam of pure, deep acid soil which has made a perfect home for an exceptional collection of calcifuge trees and shrubs.

From the pedimented façade of the house the land falls away, ornamented with a series of balustraded terraces. Thickets of evergreen *Choisya ternata* and the tender *Carpenteria californica* are planted on either side of the steps that lead down from the uppermost terrace to a paved area, with a circular pool and stone urns, which in late summer is fringed with waves of rich blue *Agapanthus* 'Headbourne Hybrid'. Running along the edges of this upper terrace are hedges of lavender which rise above lavishly planted mixed borders on either side at the lower level. A lawn now slopes down to a stream planted with moisture-loving plants such as *Gunnera manicata*. On either side woodland presses in and ornamental maples, birches and substantial shrub roses are planted in the grass where naturalised narcissi produce a great display in the spring. This arrangement produces an unforced transition from the formality of the house and its architectural terraces to the naturalistic meadow and stream.

The woodland garden on acid soil lies to one side of all this on low-lying land that is even more protected than the area about the house. Here, chiefly between the wars, a superb collection of appropriate trees and shrubs was assembled. Although no records were kept, many of these plants were propagated from seed gathered on the expeditions of George Forrest and Frank Kingdon Ward, both of whom introduced outstanding new plants in the 1920s and 1930s, chiefly from western China and Tibet. Here are the cream of the most distinguished Asiatic flowering trees and shrubs – superlative camellias, magnolias and a magnificent collection of rhododendrons. Some of the most tender plants here, however, are those from the southern hemisphere such as Winter's bark, *Drimys winteri*, and the even more beautiful *D. lanceolata* with slender leaves and rich red new growth. Further inland in Northumbria, in less protected places, tender broad-leafed evergreens such as these would stand no chance of survival. From Australasia beautiful hoherias, with felty leaves and late summer clouds of white flowers, and olearias with profuse daisy-like flowers, find a happy home. As a background to this exotic planting the ancient woodland of English oaks (*Quercus robur*) and sweet chestnuts (*Castanea sativa*) provides an exquisite background.

ABOVE *On the south terrace a lily pond lies at the centre of a vista leading across a meadow to distant views of the rural landscape. The yew hedges are splashed with scarlet* Tropaeolum speciosum.

RIGHT *Spring in the woodland garden reveals dazzling herbaceous underplanting of shrubs and trees. Pink, yellow and russet Asiatic primulas and the vivid blue of* Meconopsis betonicifolia *give colour, and the glistening mounds of the new hosta foliage make bold shapes.*

Castle Howard

orace Walpole, on visiting Castle Howard in 1772, wrote: '...nobody had informed me that I should at one view see a palace, a town, a fortified city, temples in high places, woods worthy of being each a metropolis of the Druids...the noblest lawn in the world fenced by half the horizon, and a mausoleum that would tempt one to be buried alive – In short, I have seen gigantic places before, but never a sublime one.' The scene that so struck Walpole has a similar effect on visitors today. Lord Carlisle commissioned John Vanbrugh to build his palace in this remote and wild corner of north Yorkshire in 1699. Vanbrugh, a soldier and playwright who had spent four years in a French prison on suspicion of abetting William of Orange's planned invasion of

France, was a friend of Carlisle's from the Kit-Cat Club. His commission to design Castle Howard was his first venture into architecture and the house he made for Lord Carlisle, with its attendant grandiose garden buildings, is like no other. In its spectacular setting, it assumes the role of an appropriately imposing landscape ornament.

It is likely that Vanbrugh himself had some hand in laying out the gardens but little is known for certain. Plans for a great formal garden with axial vistas, proposed by George London for the area north-east of the house known as Ray Wood, were rejected for a more naturalistic layout with paths winding through the woods; this, however, was ornamented with many statues and fountains and was far from naturalistic. It still has a

powerful atmosphere and an excellent collection of trees and shrubs planted by James Russell who came here in 1968 bringing with him the Sunningdale collection of rhododendrons. Immediately south of the house an area which had in the early 18th century been a grass parterre was replanned round the great Atlas fountain in the 1850s by W. A. Nesfield. This design was simplified, with new yew hedges, by the 9th Countess of Carlisle in the 1890s. The walled garden, formerly the kitchen garden and part of Vanbrugh's original scheme, now contains three attractive rose gardens particularly rich in the old shrub roses.

The gardens near the house are ornamental, with many excellent plants, but the real drama – what moved Walpole to refer to it as 'sublime' – takes place in the great landscape beyond. South-east of the house, high above the New River, Vanbrugh's Temple of the Four Winds forms a punctuation mark at the edge of Ray Wood. Further to the east is the great pillared and domed mausoleum begun by Nicholas Hawksmoor in 1729. West of the house Vanbrugh designed an obelisk in 1714 in honour of the Duke of Marlborough's victories, marking the junction of the two giant approaches to the house, one of which passes through an immense gatehouse crowned with a pyramid, also by Vanbrugh. These powerful monuments, animating the bleak Howardian Hills, with at their centre the house like a trumpet blast, are the most memorable scenes at Castle Howard.

OPPOSITE *Beyond the New River bridge Nicholas Hawksmoor's mausoleum rises dramatically on an eminence.*

LEFT *The Atlas fountain, with supporting Tritons, is the centrepiece of a scheme designed in the 1850s by W. A. Nesfield which replaced the early 18th-century parterre, possibly designed by Vanbrugh himself.*

Heligan

RIGHT *In the jungle garden, tree ferns (Dicksonia antarctica) have become naturalised and flourish as vigorously as they do in their native Tasmania.*

ardens do not last forever, and the larger and more complicated they are the more vulnerable they become to economic adversity or changes in horticultural fashion. There are countless examples of gardens, famous in their time, that have simply disappeared. Heligan is an instance of a great garden that has been brought back, triumphantly, from what seemed irretrievable neglect.

The Tremaynes, originally from Devon, have lived in this part of Cornwall since they came to Heligan in the 16th century. Of their earlier gardens here there is little trace but a plan of 1735 shows that there was a formal garden in front of the house before landscaping was carried out in the late 18th and early 19th centuries. The Rev. Henry Hawkins Tremayne (1766-1829) was the first of four generations of the family that made Heligan one of the finest gardens in the country. There are two aspects of the garden that give it exceptional interest. First, its climate, especially the micro-climate of the valley or 'Jungle' garden, made it a particularly suitable place to cultivate the exotic flowering shrubs that were being introduced in the 19th century. Second, Heligan was a self-contained community with its own brickworks (started in 1690, the oldest in Cornwall), brewery, several farms, sawmill, flour mill, and diverse productive gardens in which an extraordinary range of vegetables and fruit were grown.

In World War I half the staff at Heligan were killed and the estate began to decline swiftly. After the war the Tremaynes lived only briefly in the house and it was subsequently tenanted and eventually divided into flats. The gardens, still owned by the Tremaynes, were increasingly neglected. Early in 1990 a project was set up to restore the gardens and, with extraordinary speed and efficiency, money was raised and work started. The site was choked with brambles and countless fallen trees – over 700 were

blown down in the storm of January 1990 – so there was a lot to do.

Today the gardens have been transformed and their true value once again revealed. The Tremaynes had received seed from Joseph Hooker's expeditions to the Himalayas in the 1840s and 50s and some of the plants raised

still survive – for example *Rhododendron falconeri* (found by Hooker in Sikkim 1849) and *R. dalhousiae* (1848). There are also notable trees surviving from some of these early plantings. In the valley garden – which is dramatically beautiful – there is the largest *Podocarpus totara* in Britain. Even more

ABOVE *Abundant daffodils enliven woodland groves. In the background is a 19th-century brick arcade of bee boles.*

remarkable, in the same part of the garden, is a specimen of the Chinese cedar, *Cedrela sinensis* (introduced in 1862), which is over 30 metres high, taller than any known in the wild.

The walled melon garden with its various buildings – potting shed, melon house and pineapple pit – has been restored to its full glory. The pineapple pit dates back to the mid 18th century and is the only large one of its period to survive in Britain. Cultivars of pineapple known to have been grown in the 19th century are once again cultivated here. The adjacent vegetable garden is now back in full production, growing a wide range of period correct vegetables and fruit. The restoration of the walled Flower Garden with its vast glasshouses is almost complete and much of the area has already been planted. In four years of remarkable – and remarkably well-organised – work the vital spirit of Heligan has been retrieved.

Alton Towers

In the late 20th century large estates that can no longer survive in private ownership have found all kinds of different uses, some much happier than others. In the case of Alton Towers the new use, as a gigantic family theme park, has meant that the garden has not merely survived but is well cared for. Its history is relatively short and, in its own wildly romantic way, distinctly splendid.

In the middle ages there was a castle at Alton, built by the de Verdun family whose last heiress, Lady Ankarat de Verdun, married Sir John Talbot in 1412. The Talbots did not live here until the 15th Earl of Shrewsbury succeeded to the estates in 1787, by which time the castle was in ruins and the landscape a wilderness. Between 1810 and 1852, the Earl and his successors built a vast Gothic palace, employing many architects, from James Wyatt at the beginning of the project, to the great Gothicist Augustus Welby Pugin at the end. The 15th Earl, who died in 1827, was largely responsible for the garden but planting continued throughout the century.

ABOVE *The Chinese pagoda fountain in the middle of a pool was designed by Robert Abraham before 1827. Originally much more prominent, it is now enshrouded in mature woodland.*

RIGHT *The valley garden descends to ornamental pools and its slopes are profusely planted with conifers. These were first planted in the 1840s but the tradition has been maintained in the 20th century, creating an evergreen tapestry of colour.*

He chose as his site a narrow rocky valley north of the house and embarked on a prodigious scheme of planting. J. C. Loudon, visiting in 1836, wrote of the Earl: 'This nobleman, abounding in wealth, always fond of architecture and gardening, but with much more fancy than sound judgement seems to have wished to produce something different from everybody else.' In this he was entirely successful.

Even before the new castle was started, the Earl embarked on planting on a grandiose scale, with immense numbers of trees, in particular the conifers – silver firs (*Abies alba*),

Yew topiary lines the path on the terrace that leads to the conservatory. These curious shapes were planted before 1857 and have become mis-shapen and blowsy with old age.

spruce (*Picea* species), Scotch pine (*Pinus sylvestris*) – which gave a desired atmosphere of gloomy romanticism. Later on there were plantings of ornamental shrubs – camellias, rhododendrons (in 1857 'every known variety' and in 1873 'by the acre'), heathers and strawberry trees. Later still, ornamental broad-leafed trees were added such as Japanese maples (very much in evidence today) and tulip trees (*Liriodendron tulipifera*).

While all this planting was going on, ornamental buildings were being added. The architect Robert Abraham (1774-1850) was responsible for a grandiose conservatory and a Chinese pagoda surmounted by a spectacular fountain. The pagoda, designed before 1827 in the tradition of 18th-century Chinoiserie, was based on the To-Ho Pagoda in Canton,

illustrated in Sir William Chambers' *Designs of Chinese Buildings* (1757). On a rocky promontory, commanding splendid views of the gardens, Abraham also built a three-storeyed Prospect Tower (or Chinese Temple) with refined Gothic detail.

In the gardens today the original planting has become almost claustrophobically dense but, viewed from above, the colouring of varied trees and shrubs – in particular conifers, maples and heathers – makes a dazzling patchwork. The present owners, The Tussauds Group, not only maintain the gardens to high standards but have a constant programme of restoration. What was started as a private Elysium has become accessible to millions and yet its essential spirit has remained substantially intact.

Anglesey Abbey

The "abbey" was an Augustinian priory in the 12th century. After the dissolution of the monasteries in the 16th century, the building changed hands several times. In the 17th century it belonged to a Cambridge carrier, Thomas Hobson, from whose practice of hiring out horses chosen only by himself came the expression 'Hobson's choice'. Although a medieval core remains, with some 17th-century parts, most of the present house is much later, with a service wing, library and picture gallery on two floors built after 1926 when the estate was bought by Huttleston Broughton. His father, although English, had made a fortune in the USA from mining and railroads in the late 19th century. His mother, Cara Rogers, was an American heiress whose steam yacht *Sapphire* with its crew of 60 took the family on grand cruises until World War II.

Some fine trees survive at Anglesey Abbey dating back to the 1860s but the garden is almost entirely 20th century in design and conception. At 100 acres, it is probably the largest important garden made in England in this century. Furthermore, it is laid out in a unique style, an individualistic blend of the principles of 18th-century landscape gardening and the formal, baroque layouts of 17th-century France. This is a famously flat part of the country which is as unsuitable for landscape gardening as it could possibly be. The way chosen by the 1st Lord Fairhaven to animate such country was to plant avenues, open vistas and ornament the surface of the land. Several avenues were planted, some on a grand scale. The Coronation Avenue, planted south-west of the house in 1937 to celebrate the coronation of King George VI, is a quadruple alignment of horse chestnuts (*Aesculus hippocastanum*) 400 metres long forming a grand cross axis to the garden. Huttleston Broughton, who became the 1st Lord Fairhaven, built up an exceptional collection of garden sculpture and ornaments and these are deployed with skill, forming eye-catchers in the distance or standing out against dense hedges. They are satisfyingly grouped together in another feature that commemorates a royal occasion, the Temple Lawn, created in honour of the coronation of Queen Elizabeth II in 1953, which forms the terminating point of a long cross vista cutting across the Coronation Avenue. Here a circular colonnade (rescued from the demolished Chesterfield House in London) is surrounded by hedges of yew, its entrance marked by a pair of lions by John Van Nost, and a copy of Bernini's figure of David at the centre.

Nearer the house are various formal flower gardens – including a dahlia garden, a hyacinth garden, and a formal rose garden. Although the roses are perpetual flowering (a jumble of 20th-century cultivars), the other two perform for a single season; this is characteristic of the large gardens of the past, where different areas were visited only at certain times of the year. When the hyacinths die down, however, dwarf bronze-leafed dahlias, unique to Anglesey – 'Madame Stappers' (red) and 'Ella Brittain' (yellow) – are planted out. Just north of the house is an excellent herbaceous border planted in a sweeping curve backed by a beech hedge. These flower gardens seem a little arbitrary, merely dotted about with little relation to the garden as a whole. The real drama at Anglesey Abbey takes place elsewhere in the park and avenues – where grass, trees and ornaments form changing views dominated by the great East Anglian skies.

On the Temple Lawn a circle of Corinthian columns surrounds an early 20th-century copy of Bernini's 'Boy David'. Recumbent lead lions guard the entrance.

Sandringham House

NORFOLK

The estate of Sandringham was bought by the Prince of Wales, later King Edward VII, in 1861. There had been an 18th-century house which was demolished to make way for the present house which was built from 1870 onwards to the designs of A. J. Humbert, a favourite architect of the Royal Family who also did work at Frogmore and Osborne. At Sandringham he made a neo-Elizabethan mansion of red brick with pale stone dressings.

In the 1870s William Broderick Thomas laid out informal gardens west of the house and excavated a new lake. Under his direction rocks were placed by the firm Pulham & Son along its shores, according to the fashion of the time for the ornamental use of rocks. James Pulham had pioneered the use of Portland cement, often mixed with industrial clinker, to make cheap and easily shaped artificial stone to meet the growing demand for rock work. He called this material 'Pulhamite' and at Sandringham it was used by this upper lake, mixed with carstone – the local 'gingerbread stone' of a distinctive yellow-brown colour. On the north shore the grotto-boathouse is roofed with Pulhamite.

The Norwich Gates, to the north of the house, also date from the first years of the garden. These magnificent cast- and wrought-iron gates were made for the International Exhibition of 1862 by Thomas Jeckell and bought by the gentry of Norfolk as a wedding present for Edward and Alexandra, Prince and Princess of Wales, in 1863.

There was much tree planting in the late 19th and early 20th centuries, particularly of conifers. Many Scots pines, Wellingtonias (*Sequiadendron giganteum*) – among the tallest in the country – deodars (*Cedrus deodarus*), and dwarf conifers by the lake give a characteristic high Victorian flavour. As shown by the heathland, so strikingly visible in these parts, this is acid country and azaleas and rhododendrons are well represented. Although the general character of the gardens is of an informal, naturalistic kind, there are excellent formal gardens immediately to the north of the house. Here in 1947 Sir Geoffrey Jellicoe laid out a satisfying symmetrical arrangement of a path flanked by pleached limes leading to a geometric pattern of abundantly planted box-edged borders. This decorative neo-classical garden was commissioned by King George VI whose rooms overlooked it. At the head of the pleached lime walk, to one side, is a curious Chinese bronze figure of the Buddhist divinity Kuvera, flanked by stone lion-dogs.

Since 1968, a large part of the estate (some 600 acres) has been set aside as a country park. Previously mostly heathland, this area has been enriched by a programme of tree planting, providing habitats for a wide range of flora and fauna. It is now open to the public every day of the year. The gardens open frequently and offer the public a rare chance to see a garden of the Royal Family on an appropriately grand scale.

RIGHT *A spawling juniper (Juniperus × media 'Pfitzeriana') contrasts with ornamental rock.*

OPPOSITE *The shores of the upper lake, below the west façade of the house, are fringed with ornamental trees and conifers planted among rocks.*

Duncombe Park

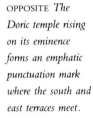Very few historic gardens have such an immediate power to astonish and delight the visitor as Duncombe Park. In some places, teasing out the history gradually reveals the interest of a site and gives us the understanding to make something of it. At

likely that he had the advice of Sir John Vanbrugh whose spirit suffuses the place. The garden, together with its dramatic terracing, was made very shortly afterwards.

The site chosen for the house was on high land, on the edge of the market town of

marking the beginning of the perfectly straight south terrace which doubles sharply back to intersect the Broadwalk which runs past the eastern façade of the house. Both terraces are of closely mown turf with billowing clumps of yew and box on one side

OPPOSITE *The Doric temple rising on its eminence forms an emphatic punctuation mark where the south and east terraces meet.*

LEFT *Parterres were created at either end of the house when wings were added by Sir Charles Barry in 1843. This shows the south parterre with an 18th-century statue of Flora in the background.*

Duncombe history certainly adds to one's appreciation but the spirit of the place speaks out loud and clear.

The great founder of the family fortunes was Sir Charles Duncombe, a banker in the City and Lord Mayor of London in 1708. He bought the Helmsley estate from the Duke of Buckingham in 1689, earning a lofty rebuke from Alexander Pope – 'And Helmsley, once proud Buckingham's delight/Slides to a Scrivener or City Knight.' When Sir Charles died unmarried in 1711, his niece inherited, changing her husband's name from Browne to Duncombe. The house we see today was probably already started, for it is illustrated in *Vitruvius Britannicus* (1713). It was designed by a gentleman architect, William Wakefield, who came from nearby Easingwold, but it is

Helmsley with its spectacular ruined 13th-century castle. On one side lay fertile plains and on the other a brisk descent to the valley of the Rye. Sometime before 1730 the land to the south and the east of the house was shaped into two giant terraces. The east terrace curves round to embrace a sharp meander of the river below. At each end is a classical temple, both of which were built in about 1730. To the north an open Ionic rotunda, possibly designed by Vanbrugh and almost identical to one designed by him for Stowe, has exquisite views of the ruined castle and the rooftops of Helmsley. All along the east terrace are beautiful views of the curving river, and a glimpse of a broad formal cascade to the east. At the southern end a Doric temple sits on top of a grassy mound,

and on the other a downward slope edged in clipped beech hedges. The visitor may walk along these terraces today, viewing scenery of exquisite beauty, scarcely changed since the 18th century. The Duncombes later built a similar terrace, with temples and a grassy walk, at Rievaulx three miles away, overlooking the remains of the great Cistercian abbey.

There is much else to see at Duncombe, including magnificent trees; by Mill Bridge, for example, is the tallest common lime (*Tilia × europaea*) in Britain, at over 46 metres high. There are also attractive Victorian parterres at either end of the house and a pretty 19th-century conservatory. But the unforgettable feature of Duncombe is the stately progress along the terraces from temple to temple and the lovely views below.

Chatsworth

Since at least the 17th century the house and garden at Chatsworth have been subjects of awe-struck admiration. Charles Cotton in his poem 'Wonders of the Peak' (1681) came to the conclusion '*That this is* Paradice, *which seated stands/In the midst of* Desarts *and of barren* Sands'. The

designers of the day. William Stukeley saw the new gardens shortly after their completion and recorded: 'The gardens abound with green-houses, summer-houses, walks, wildernesses, oranges, with all the furniture of statues, urns, greens etc. with canals, basins, and waterworks of various

Cavendishes came from Suffolk and built their first house in 1552, choosing an exquisite site on the slopes of the wide valley of the Derwent. By the time Charles Cotton was writing, the Elizabethan house was about to be engulfed in a spectacular programme of rebuilding initiated by the 4th Earl of Devonshire, with major contributions from William Talman, the court architect to William III. Kip's engraving of 1707 shows the results: a palatial baroque mansion set in grandiose formal gardens laid out by George London and Henry Wise, the greatest garden

forms.' One of the waterworks was a spectacular formal cascade with a superb water temple designed by Thomas Archer, with water flowing dramatically down its dome. This survives today, as does much of the layout of London and Wise's formal gardens although most of the details are lost. Also surviving from this time is an elegant conservatory, built in 1698, which now houses a collection of camellias and is the centrepiece of a rose garden.

The 4th Duke of Devonshire, like many of his fashionable contemporaries, engaged

ABOVE *The Sea Horse Fountain, with Triton blasting water into the air, was carved by Caius Gabriel Cibber between 1688 and 1691. Pleached limes on either side, in the style of the original 17th-century formal garden, were added in the 1950s.*

LEFT *The ring pond has a fountain at the centre with a 17th-century lead figure of a duck. The rondel of beech hedges is embellished with a series of 18th-century stone busts removed in the 1930s from another Devonshire estate, Chiswick House in London. From the pond two crinkle-crankle beech hedges climb up the hill into woodland.*

Capability Brown in 1760 to landscape the park and make alterations to the garden. He removed some of the formal gardens south-east of the house and made the Great Slope (now called the Salisbury Lawns), a great lawn joining the house to naturalistic woodland. When Horace Walpole visited in 1768 he found the gardens 'much improved… many foolish waterworks being taken away, oaks & rocks taken into the garden, & a magnificent bridge built'.

In 1826 the 6th Duke recruited Joseph Paxton as his head gardener and together they carried out alterations and made additions on a grand scale: a vast rock garden – 'the most picturesque assemblage of natural rocks' as Paxton called it; a great conservatory designed in conjunction with Decimus Burton; a pinetum made in the 1830s to provide a home for the many new conifers which were being introduced; a great fountain in the canal pond, made in 1843 in honour of a proposed visit by Tsar Nicholas of Russia who, alas, never came. Paxton remained at Chatsworth for over 30 years and was the epitome of a head gardener in an age when gardening was taken seriously. He became a director of the Midland Railway and Member of Parliament for Coventry and was duly knighted.

In present times not only is the garden beautifully cared for, but the Duchess of Devonshire (the wife of the 11th Duke), herself a keen gardener, has added much: a pair of crinkle-crankle beech hedges, a yew maze, exuberant borders and a charming miniature garden. It is this continuing vitality overlaid on the brilliant survivals of the past that gives Chatsworth its particular excitement.

Blenheim Palace

*V*oltaire famously said of Blenheim Palace that it was 'une grosse masse de pierre, sans agrément et sans goût' ('a great heap of stone, tasteless and without charm'). Others have agreed with Voltaire's view of the palace but few would deny the charms of the gardens which are among the most attractive and historically rich of any great house in England. The palace – the only non-royal palace in the country – was built from 1705 onwards by Sir John Vanbrugh and Nicholas Hawksmoor for the Duke of Marlborough. From the start it was conceived, in Vanbrugh's own words, as both 'a private habitation' and 'a National Monument' which should have 'the qualities proper to such a monument, viz., Beauty, Magnificence and Duration'.

The gardens at Blenheim were planned at the same time as the house and Henry Wise, master gardener to Queen Anne, was recruited in 1705 to lay out a scheme in keeping with the ambitions of the palace. These, too, were thought of as a monument and as a celebration of Marlborough's great victory over Louis XIV at Blenheim on the Danube. South-east of the palace Wise devised a grandiose formal garden, with a 230-metre parterre, followed by a formal hexagonal wilderness extending for almost 800 metres away from the palace, planted with bay, holly, laurel and yew and interlaced with winding paths. The whole was enclosed by walls punctuated with raised military bastions from which visitors could look down and admire the dazzling vistas of evergreens

ABOVE *A lead version of the much-copied classical Greek figure of a warrior in Achille Duchêne's neo-classical water parterre made in the 1920s.*

OPPOSITE *The Italian parterre was laid out in 1908 with patterns of clipped box, ordinary and golden, embellished with Tuscan terracotta pots filled with fuchsias and pelargoniums.*

and sparkling fountains. South-east of the formal gardens Vanbrugh and Wise created a vast kitchen garden, at a slight angle so as to present walls that faced due south, and this too was given a military character with bastions 30 metres across. In 1716 Vanbrugh wrote to the Duke of Marlborough: 'The Kitchen Garden, now the trees are in full vigour and full of fruit, is really an astonishing sight. All I ever saw in England or abroad are trifles to it.'

All this was cleared away when Capability Brown landscaped the gardens in the 1760s.

North-west of the palace he dammed the little river Glyme to make a curving lake, but left a narrow section in the middle to retain Vanbrugh's Grand Bridge. Aligned with the bridge, sweeping up the hill, was a quadruple avenue of elms, now replanted with limes. They led to the brow of the hill where a Doric column 40 metres high stood, built between 1727 and 1730 and crowned by a statue of Marlborough holding a winged victory 'as an ordinary man might hold a bird'. All this, incidentally, is a good example of Brown retaining older formal elements in his designs and making them an essential part of his new composition.

In more recent times the most striking addition to the gardens has been the neo-classical schemes of the Frenchman Achille Duchêne. Starting in 1908 he created an elegant Italian garden on the south-east corner of the palace with a fountain made by the sculptor Waldo Story. In the same position, to the south-west of the palace, Duchêne added between 1925 and 1930 the Water Terrace gardens – in precisely the position in which Vanbrugh and Hawksmoor had suggested placing a water garden.

The visitor to Blenheim today will enter the park through Hawksmoor's Triumphal Arch in the village of Woodstock. The view is exactly that of Turner's watercolour of about 1832, with Brown's gentle slopes falling to Vanbrugh's bridge that spans the lake and the palace, every inch a monument, rising magnificently on the brow of the hill.

Haddon Hall

The hall is built on a bluff overlooking water meadows on the banks of the meandering river Wye from which mists often rise to veil the medieval buildings. The resulting light, saturated with moisture, intensifies the colour of the flowers.

Sir Nikolaus Pevsner wrote: 'Haddon Hall is the English castle par excellence, not the forbidding fortress on an unassailable crag, but the large, rambling, safe, grey, lovable house of knights and their ladies.' Lovable is not the word that normally springs to mind in connection with castles but Pevsner vividly evokes the charm of the place. Only a few miles away from Chatsworth, it is very different in design and atmosphere. Its history is astonishingly ancient, going back to the late 12th century when Richard de Vernon was granted permission to fortify, and much of the wall he built survives today. The vast bulk of the castle as we see it today was built in the 14th and 15th centuries. The estate passed by the marriage of the heiress Dorothy Vernon to Sir John Manners in the 16th century, whose direct descendant, the 10th Duke of Rutland, lives there today. It was the present Duke's father who was responsible for restoring the gardens to their current state.

Haddon Hall is marvellously sited on a wooded outcrop overlooking the river Wye which at this point is a mere stream. The history of the gardens is not especially well documented, although it is known that fruit and vegetables were grown here from earliest times. When Celia Fiennes visited Haddon in 1697 she thought it 'a good old house' and wrote of 'good gardens but nothing very curious as the mode now is'. What she found old fashioned was precisely what, much later on, attracted the Arts and Crafts architects to Haddon Hall. The architect and garden designer H. Inigo Triggs did measured drawings of the gardens in 1901 and wrote in *Formal Gardens in England and Scotland* that it

'so well demonstrates the importance of considering a house and garden as one design'. This unity is something of which the garden visitor today is strikingly aware.

The gardens in their present form date from the late 16th century and consist of a series of terraces and courtyards immediately adjacent to the castle walls to the south and east and intimately connected to the castle. The six terraces provide wonderfully sympathetic spaces for planting which today is dominated by an immense collection of roses of every kind – ranging from perpetual-flowering modern roses to old shrub roses. The castle walls and the balustrades edging

In the terraced gardens roses are used profusely, looking magnificent against the old stone of the walls and balustrades. Here the richly scented rambler, Rosa 'Albertine', flanks steps leading up from the middle terrace to Dorothy Vernon's walk.

terraces and staircases, make perfect places for climbing roses which look marvellous against the old grey stone.

Other plantings greatly extend the flowering season. In early spring the first narcissus appear followed by many tulips. Other climbing plants, in particular clematis, flower from spring to autumn and in summer intermingle with the roses. Immediately below the south-facing wall of the castle in the Fountain Terrace below the windows of the long gallery a bed is filled with many delphiniums attractively underplanted with *Viola cornuta*. A long herbaceous border faces west at the back of Dorothy Vernon's Walk and the high retaining wall above it is festooned with climbing plants.

The gardens at Haddon are on a modest scale for a house of such splendour and historical resonance. Their warm and welcoming enclosures trap any sun and the planting, far from being overawed by such a setting, is boisterously friendly rather than cold and formal.

St Paul's Walden Bury

HERTFORDSHIRE

St Paul's Walden Bury is one of a small group of surviving formal gardens, which includes Melbourne Hall and Bramham Park, that date from the early years of the 18th century. This gives them a particular historical interest but it also happens that they are especially attractive gardens. St Paul's Walden Bury, in a surprisingly rural corner of Hertfordshire near the Bedfordshire border, preserves a wonderfully unspoilt character. The house, partly neo-classical of the 1760s (possibly by James Paine) and partly Victorian neo-Elizabethan, replaced a house of the 1730s which was contemporary with the formal garden. This earlier house had been built for Edward Gilbert and had passed to his daughter Mrs Mary Bowes. The estate has remained in the family (later Bowes Lyon) ever since.

The garden that Edward Gilbert made was distinctly old fashioned for its time. It was, and remains to this day, in essence an English vision of a French baroque garden. From the garden front of the house a *patte d'oie* of radiating avenues sweeps downwards. The central *allée* is broader and much longer than the other two and all three are lined with beech hedges (*Fagus sylvatica*). Behind the hedges, woodland presses in providing views of a more naturalistic landscape than any 17th-century French garden would allow. Nor would any French classical garden designer have been happy with the undulating site which gives the *allées* a sinuous rise and fall, so attractive to the English eye. Each of the three vistas of the *patte d'oie* has an eye-catcher – the central one a figure of Hercules, another a figure of Diana and the third, an attractive example of 'borrowed landscape', the spire of the village church of All Saints. Although this layout has survived, it has undergone a great deal of embellishment in the 20th century.

In 1932 the Hon. David Bowes Lyon, who was a great gardener, plant collector and, from 1953 to 1961, President of the Royal

Horticultural Society, took charge of the garden. With advice from Geoffrey Jellicoe he restored the existing layout and introduced various decorative garden buildings. These have been sympathetically worked into the existing design which has, here and there, been subtly modified to accommodate them. They include a handsome 18th-century domed temple brought from Copped Hall and placed at the western end of a vista that cuts across the *patte d'oie*, and, at the eastern end, on the far side of a lake, a temple rescued from Danson Hall in Kent. To one side of the central *allée*, half-hidden among the trees, is a grassy amphitheatre with a temple on an eminence and a pool overlooked by a copy of a Greek statue of a warrior known here as 'The Running Footman'.

Outside the formal garden there is ornamental planting with many flowering shrubs: eucryphias, hydrangeas, magnolias and rhododendrons are prominent. These do not intrude on the formal layout, but provide decorative interludes in the surrounding woodland. However, it is the enchanting pattern of *allées*, statues and temples that is truly memorable.

ABOVE *The front lawn is ornamented with pleached lime alleys on either side. On the west side is a fine copy of Giambologna's statue of Hercules and Antaeus.*

RIGHT *An 18th-century temple, possibly designed by Sir William Chambers, was moved in the 1950s from a garden in Kent to this prominent position on the banks of the lake.*

alemain has a marvellous position overlooking the broad valley of the river Eamont which flows out of the eastern end of Ullswater. The present external appearance of the house, built in lovely pink-silver sandstone, dates chiefly from the mid 18th century, but parts of it go back much further, even as early as the 12th century. The estate was bought in the late 17th century by the Hasell family whose descendants still live there.

Very shortly after Sir Edward Hasell came to Dalemain he started work on the garden. In 1685 he recruited the help of James Swingler, of Dutch origin, who had come to East Anglia to advise on draining the fens. Part of his work at Dalemain was to enclose the garden and an orchard in stone walls and to lay out the planting. In the early 18th century Sir Edward's son landscaped the parkland around the house and formed an ornamental lake by damming the river Eamont. An early Georgian summerhouse,

built into the garden walls and containing Chippendale-style seats, also survives from this period. Later in the century there was much planting of trees and there is a record in 1782 of several named varieties of apple trees, including the local Keswick Codlin, a cooking apple ('tender, soft and very juicy') bred by the nurseryman John Sander of Keswick. In the late 19th century, William Stuart, the head gardener, held sway for 50 years and ran the garden to perfectionist standards.

In the last 20 years the garden has undergone a splendid renaissance in the hands of its owners. Sylvia Hasell, the daughter of the last of the line, married Bryce McCosh and they boldly decided to open the garden at Dalemain to the public as a way of helping to make the estate self-supporting. Mrs McCosh, who had known the garden as a child when Mr Stuart was head gardener and had learnt much from him, immensely enriched the planting and raised standards of maintenance

to a high degree. This work is continued today by her daughter-in-law Jane Hasell McCosh.

The terrace garden adjacent to the house has a gravel walk running along a deep, well-established herbaceous border with rudbeckia, delphiniums, phlox, hardy geraniums, ligularia, penstemons and verbascums. The stone wall behind is planted with climbing roses, among them the splendidly blowsy golden-yellow 'Easlea's Golden Rambler' and 'Emily Gray' with exceptionally decorative glossy foliage. The walk leads past a fine Grecian fir (*Abies cephalonica*) to the more intimate character of the Elizabethan garden. Here low box hedges enclose miniature beds planted with *Ruta graveolens*, alliums, lilies, *Viola cornuta*, cotton lavender and agapanthus. A path leads round the walled garden which contains shrub roses and fruit trees, and, in one corner, a pretty Tudor gazebo or garden house. A door leads out of the north wall into Lobb's Wood where a winding path has exquisite views over Dacre Beck.

The garden which the McCosh family has made, with the advantage of an exceptional site possessing rich historical patina, has a kind of unforced charm, appropriate to its setting and entirely sympathetic to visitors.

LEFT *In the upper part of the walled garden a mixed border runs along the wall with old apple trees. Here many shrub roses ('Constance Spry' on the left) are skilfully underplanted with herbaceous plants including, earlier in the season, a fine bed of brilliant blue Himalayan poppies (*Meconopsis betonicifolia) which relish the acid soil.*

OPPOSITE *The Elizabethan garden has a box-edged knot garden. Planting is bold and simple with blocks of a single plant – rue (*Ruta graveolens), santolina, white *Viola cornuta *and the grey-leafed perennial wallflower* Erysimum *'Bowle's Mauve'.*

Nymans

Nymans is distinguished not only by its planting, which includes many great rarities, but also by its strong and lively, essentially 20th-century design. It is largely the creation of a single family – the Messels – which over four generations has lavished care on the garden. Ludwig Messel bought the estate in 1890 and between 1925 and 1930 his son Leonard replaced the early 19th-century house with what Ian Nairn in *The Buildings of England* describes as an 'amazingly deceptive evocation of a major manor house of the C14 to the C16'. It was designed by Sir Walter Tapper and largely destroyed by fire after World War II but its gaunt and gabled remains have a monumental presence in the gardens.

The first part of the garden which Ludwig Messel laid out was the Wall Garden, the former kitchen garden shaped like a stirrup. The curved south-facing wall is found in many 18th-century kitchen gardens – there is a similar one not far away at William Robinson's Gravetye Manor. The Wall Garden is in many ways a précis of the atmosphere of the whole garden, mixing refined design with fastidious plantsmanship. A cruciform arrangement of paths divides the area into four, their meeting point marked by an Italian red marble fountain surrounded by four drums of clipped yew surmounted by topiary coronets. The path that runs roughly north-south is lined with double mixed borders originally planted by James Comber, Ludwig Messel's head gardener. Their design has been attributed, with no firm evidence, to both William Robinson and Gertrude Jekyll. These are borders for high summer and much use is made of bold tender perennials such as *Canna indica* 'Purpurea' as well as many carefully chosen annuals which change slightly from year to year, always maintaining a lively colour scheme but avoiding excessively strident pinks and oranges. Behind these borders is a completely different atmosphere. Here, marvellous ornamental trees and shrubs, some rather tender and benefiting from the walled protection, are planted in informal profusion and underplanted with spring bulbs such as erythroniums and fritillaries. *Styrax japonica* is here, one of the best small deciduous trees for a protected site in neutral-to-acid soil. It has hanging bell-shaped white flowers in early summer followed by decorative acorn-like fruit and lovely warm yellow autumn foliage. Here too are several magnolias, the beautiful eucryphia bred here, *E. × nymansensis*, and the North American fringe tree *Chionanthus virginicus*. Many of these are rarities, all are beautiful.

Over the years the Messels expanded the garden adding a very wide variety of features. The pinetum was planted in the 1890s but almost obliterated by the great storm of 1987. Much replanting has been done, often with plants propagated from trees lost in the storm. The Top Garden was started in about 1910 and has mixed borders and excellent trees and shrubs – dogwoods, magnolias, rowans and southern beeches. A rose garden dates from the 1920s when Miss Willmott presented a collection of old shrub roses. This was replanted recently and looks very handsome underplanted with hardy geraniums.

Few gardens suffered more in the storm of 1987 but although many large old specimens were lost, the recovery has been remarkably swift and well organised and the garden is once more brimming with confidence.

Yew hedges shaped into dramatic castellations frame the dovecote and echo the gabled architecture of the house.

Caerhays Castle

CORNWALL

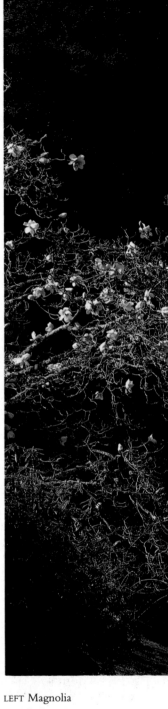

The castle at Caerhays was built in 1808, to the designs of John Nash, for the Trevanion family – a 'very picturesque castellated mansion in a superb position' as Sir Nikolaus Pevsner describes it. The estate was bought in 1852 by Michael Williams whose family, from Wales but resident in Cornwall since the 18th century, became one of the most important of the Cornish gardening dynasties. Michael Williams came from Scorrier House near Redruth which had been built by his grandfather in 1778. This had a distinguished garden noted for its trees and described in *The Garden* in 1881 as having 'one of the finest and best managed Camellia walks in England'. The Williamses also had excellent gardens at Burncoose and at Tregullow (both still owned by the family and still full of interest).

Caerhays Castle is built on an eminence facing south towards Porthluney Cove and the sea. Behind the castle the land slopes briskly upwards and its wooded heights give protection from the coldest winds. Between the entrance lodge and the castle a sinuous lake spreads out to the east. It has been suggested that this was the work of Humphry Repton but there is no conclusive evidence. Repton was certainly in partnership with John Nash – and Repton had made one of his most beautiful landscapes not very far away at Antony House.

The distinction of the garden is chiefly owed to John Charles Williams who, from 1897 onwards, built up a very remarkable collection of plants, taking advantage of an exceptionally privileged micro-climate and a most beautiful site. He was one of the most important supporters of the plant-hunting expeditions of George Forrest who, from 1904 onwards, introduced many distinguished plants from China. Among these were over 300 new rhododendrons and several camellias including *C. saluensis* which was crossed at Caerhays in the 1920s with *C. japonica* to form the *C × williamsii* hybrid

which has produced many outstanding cultivars. J. C. Williams subscribed to other important expeditions of his day including those of Reginald Farrer, Frank Kingdon-Ward and E. H. Wilson. It was Wilson who discovered in 1908 the exquisite small Chinese rhododendron *R. williamsianum* named in Williams' honour.

As this flood of new plants arrived at Caerhays, clearings were made in the woodland to accommodate them. Apart from the camellias and rhododendrons, the other group of Asiatic flowering shrubs best

RIGHT *An immense* Magnolia campbellii *soars over the castle gatehouse on the right of which are ramparts of camellias.*

LEFT Magnolia campbellii *was introduced from the Himalayas in 1865. Those at Caerhays are among the largest in the country.*

represented is the magnolia. One of the best of George Forrest's introductions was *M. campbellii* ssp. *mollicomata* which produces its enormous, rich mauve-pink flowers very early in the season. At Caerhays there remain some specimens propagated from the first seed sent by Forrest from Yunnan in 1924.

Another Forrest introduction (1918), which first flowered in this country at Caerhays, is the exquisite, evergreen, magnolia-like *Michelia doltsopa* with its headily-scented white flowers. This very tender plant is scarcely seen in England outside Cornwall.

Caerhays is primarily a plant collection but the planting is arranged in a very natural fashion, taking every advantage of the lovely site. The visitor, wandering from marvel to marvel, will experience something of the excitement of the plant hunters first coming upon some new wonder in the densely planted jungle.

The Savill Garden

SURREY

This is the only garden in this book, and as far as I know in this country, named after its maker. Eric Savill (Sir Eric from 1955) worked for the family firm of chartered surveyors and in 1931 was appointed Deputy Surveyor of Windsor Park and Woods. Windsor Park is one of the most ancient of all royal estates dating back to William the Conqueror who took over a Saxon hunting lodge very near the present site of Windsor castle. There was a Great Garden at Windsor and records survive of royal gardeners from early on; for example, from as early as 1296, when Adam the Gardener was 'Gardener of the King's Garden within the Castle'. Windsor Great Park was a

transformed its appearance with the planting of huge numbers of trees and a programme of drainage. The picturesque streams and lakes seen today are as often as not part of a system of drainage which changed vast areas of bog and heath into fertile, cultivable soil.

When Eric Savill was appointed there was an estate nursery on the eastern boundary of the Great Park and it was here that he proposed to create a woodland garden. This is not dramatic scenery but there is an attractive rise and fall of land and the priceless attraction of streams and ponds. The Royal Family took a keen interest in these new developments from early on – after inspecting it King George V and Queen Mary are reported to

piece of managed landscape from at least the 16th century when there are records of oak planting. Much later, in the middle of the 18th century, the Duke of Cumberland made an exotic landscape garden at Virginia Water, very near the Savill Garden, with buildings by Henry Flitcroft. The Duke of Cumberland was Ranger of Windsor Great Park and

have said 'It is very small Mr Savill, but very nice'. The garden grew – it now occupies 35 acres – and became an exceptional collection, particularly of trees and shrubs.

The soil here is acid and ericaceous plants are well represented with formidable numbers of azaleas, camellias and rhododendrons. These are often planted among old forest

ABOVE *The Jubilee Bridge spans the stream whose banks are edged with plants chosen for their decorative autumn colour and fruits.*

LEFT *Autumn foliage – the scarlet leaves of* Cotinus coggygria *and butter-yellow leaves of a Norway maple – blowing in the wind.*

trees – in particular beautiful oaks – and intermingled with smaller ornamental trees such as dogwoods and Japanese maples. This style of planting is often called naturalistic but, quite apart from the fact that countless of the plants are garden varieties, nature never grew such a wide range of plants in a single site. But the dense planting, often with a rich underplanting of herbaceous plants and bulbs, laced with winding paths, certainly produces a sympathetic vision of idealised nature.

Although it is the woody plants that are the most immediately striking feature, there are excellent herbaceous plants (especially of moisture-loving kinds running along the banks of the stream) and beautifully kept herbaceous borders. The Savill Garden has also taken an active role in the conservation of garden plants. In conjunction with the nearby Valley Garden, also in Windsor Great Park, several National Collections are held including those of dwarf conifers, hollies, magnolias, mahonias, pernettyas, pieris and species rhododendrons.

Clare College

CAMBRIDGESHIRE

In the centre of Cambridge the colleges that run along the east bank of the Cam, with splendid views over the wooded Backs, enjoy a setting that has all the Arcadian charms of an 18th-century landscape park. The best of them also possess their own private gardens, some hidden away within secluded courts, others flaunting themselves in prominent positions along the river bank. Clare College has all these advantages and in addition the setting of its own beautiful buildings and the borrowed landscapes of neighbouring colleges – in particular the great chapel of King's College alongside.

Although a 14th-century foundation, Clare College was entirely rebuilt in the 17th and 18th centuries. Its position in relation to the river, and the deliberate visual connection between Old Court, the bridge over the Cam and a continuing vista towards Queen's Road, show a remarkable sensitivity to its setting. From Old Court the visitor passes through a grand early 17th-century arch which leads to the bridge of the same date which is ornamented with sea-horses and Arion riding a dolphin. From the bridge, looking back towards the College, there are glimpses through iron railings of the closed gardens of the Master's Lodge – a flash of green lawn and bold borders.

The Fellows' Garden lies on the other side of the river, immediately to the north of a straight avenue that leads from the bridge. This was already an enclosed garden in 1688 but the present layout was created immediately after World War II. It was designed by Professor Neville Willmer who contrived a satisfying mixture of formality and informality in which lawns and fine specimen trees are interspersed with more artful decorative interludes. Among the trees are a huge swamp cypress (*Taxodium distichum*), a pocket handkerchief tree (*Davidia involucrata*) and an old example of a tree frequently seen in Cambridge, the Judas tree (*Cercis siliquastrum*). A pair of outstanding herbaceous borders is planted in a colour scheme restricted to blue-purple and yellow. The detail is subtly contrived: a central path of gravel is edged with strips of fine turf and the path leads towards a narrow gap in crisp yew hedges clipped with sloping tops. Beyond, a formal sunken water garden has an Arts and Crafts flavour with walls of fine old brick and tall Italian cypresses rising over a formal pool with scalloped ends. Professor Willmer had a special interest in colour perception and in the blue-purple and yellow borders, and bold borders of orange and red that run along the Cam, he was able to display the powerful effects of harmonious colour planting.

The eye-catcher at the end of the axial vista that leads through the trees from the bridge, is a magnificent set of wrought-iron gates – 'supreme amongst Cambridge ironwork' as Pevsner wrote – leading out into Queen's Road. On the far side of Queen's Road the gardens of Memorial Court in the new Clare College building have some excellent trees (including a splendid Caucasian wingnut, *Pterocarya fraxinifolia*) and sculptures by Barbara Hepworth and Henry Moore.

LEFT *Much use is made of bedding plants and restricted colour schemes. Ramparts of white antirrhinums and white lilies make a cool border in part-shade beside a winding gravel path.*

OPPOSITE *In the herbaceous borders colours are restricted to blue-purple and yellow. Tall yellow verbascums and deep blue delphiniums soar above heleniums, catmint and blue scabious.*

Holker Hall

olker Hall is splendidly sited on the wooded slopes of the Cartmel peninsula which juts out from the north into Morecambe Bay. Formerly part of the Cartmel Priory estate, it was acquired by the Preston family shortly after the dissolution of the monasteries in the 16th century. Since then it has belonged to two other families only, passing by inheritance to the Lowthers and to the Cavendishes who live there today. The house suffered two great fires in the 19th century and the present appearance of the new wing, a very handsome neo-Elizabethan mansion of lovely rose-coloured stone, is chiefly the work in the 1870s of the Lancashire architects Paley and Austin.

The history of the gardens starts in the early 18th century when Sir Thomas Lowther laid out a formal scheme in the fashionable style of the day with statues despatched by sea from London in 1729. This garden was obliterated late in the 18th century by Lord George Cavendish who replaced it with 200 acres of 'natural' parkland, planting some fine new trees, including cedars of Lebanon (*Cedrus libani libani*) of which one superb specimen survives. In the 1840s Lord George's grandson, the 7th Duke of Devonshire, sought advice on the garden from Sir Joseph Paxton who had been head gardener at Chatsworth under the 6th Duke. Several new features were added: an arboretum (which included the monkey puzzle, *Araucaria araucana*, recently introduced from Chile); a conservatory; balustraded terraces by the house and a large walled kitchen garden. In the early 20th century a rose garden and pergola were commissioned from the Arts and Crafts designer Thomas Mawson.

Throughout the 20th century the scale and interest of the planting has developed, and Holker is now one of the most worthwhile gardens to visit in the north of England. With its acid soil, very high rainfall but benign climate, it provides ideal conditions for the conifers, first planted under Sir Joseph Paxton, and for the rhododendrons, some of which derive from Hooker's introductions of the late 19th century. Many other trees and shrubs also relish these exceptional conditions – dogwoods, enkianthus, eucryphias, hoherias, magnolias, maples and stewartias. The woods are rich in bulbs and the formal areas about the house, with their handsome architectural setting, are skilfully planted. A characteristic late 20th-century feature is the interest in conservation, shown in particular in two parts of the garden. In the meadow garden the grass is cut very late to allow the seeding of diverse pasture herbs, and more exotic plants such as martagon lilies have become naturalised. In the woodland garden the National Collection of the family *Styracaceae* is conserved and includes some of the most beautiful of the Asiatic flowering trees, among them the exquisite *Styrax japonica*.

All historic gardens possess interesting features that survive from earlier times. The most exciting examples, however, such as Holker Hall, also show signs of a continuing liveliness of horticultural interest which adds immeasurably to the delights of the past.

ABOVE *The Italian fountain in the woodland garden is encircled by paving and beautifully laid miniature cobbles. The sprawling trunk of a 100-year-old rhododendron* (R. arboreum), *with its textured bark, is strikingly decorative.*

RIGHT *The formal gardens by the house have lavish ornamental planting. Above beds of* Alchemilla mollis, *artemisia, lavender and violets, standard-trained Portugal laurel (Prunus lusitanica) and stone urns give structural emphasis.*

Bicton Park Gardens

DEVON

Bicton is an anciently inhabited place – with evidence of a medieval deer park – but its detailed history starts in the 18th century. The mansion house was rebuilt by James Wyatt in about 1800 for the Rolle family who had come into the estate by marriage in the 17th century. In the early 20th century the house was remodelled by the architect Sir Walter Tapper who gave it its present neo-Georgian appearance.

In the early 18th century, under Henry Rolle, M.P. for Barnstaple and the 1st Lord Rolle of Stevenstone, the Italian Garden was laid out at some distance south of the house. This garden has been attributed to André le Nôtre, but there is no evidence. Le Nôtre died in 1700 and it is not known that he ever came to England; nor is there, apart from its formal, axial design and use of water, any obvious similarity to known le Nôtre schemes. The garden consists of grassy terraces with a rectangular pool and canal running across the axis, overlooked by Irish yews and statues of the period, with the whole aligned on an obelisk far to the south.

The northern end of the Italian garden now has a distinctly 19th-century flavour with fountains and borders planted with bedding plants. A range of Victorian glass-houses is decorated with busts of Sir Walter

The Italian Garden was laid out in the early 18th century with a canal and fine statues of Arcadian figures. The ground is sculpted into dramatic turf-covered slopes.

In late summer the decorative seed pods of honesty (Lunaria annua) and tobacco plants (Nicotiana glauca) continue to provide interest in a mixed border.

Raleigh and Lord Nelson. To the west, beyond the perimeter of the Italian garden, is one of the earliest and most beautiful surviving glasshouses, the Palm House. It was built in about 1820 by the London firm of W. & D. Bailey, using the curvilinear glazed roof invented by J. C. Loudon who had built an experimental glasshouse along the same lines at his garden in Bayswater. The Palm House is in three parts, its curved roof soaring upwards like billowing sails, exquisitely fashioned out of a thin metal framework glazed in slender panes of glass. It has recently been restored and attractively planted.

In the grounds that surround the house – now the home of the Devon College of Agriculture – there is also a pronounced 19th-century character. The entrance drive

has a splendid avenue of monkey puzzle trees (*Araucaria araucana*) planted in 1842 with the advice of James Veitch, the great Exeter nurseryman. The monkey puzzle was first introduced to England in any quantity in 1839; Veitch's nursery advertised them for sale in 1843 in the *Gardeners' Chronicle*, having raised 'many thousands from seed'. The avenue at Bicton is, therefore, one of the earliest and best surviving groups of this most characteristic of early Victorian trees. The parkland near the house, especially to the south and east, is rich in fine trees of a much

earlier date, for example a group of superb sweet chestnuts (*Castanea sativa*) that dates from the mid 18th century. There are many excellent oaks, including a magnificent Lucombe oak (*Quercus × hispanica* 'Lucombeana' 'William Lucombe'), over 30 metres high, named after the 18th-century Exeter nurseryman who raised the original tree in 1763 from which this was probably propagated. It is encouraging that there is much new tree planting in these parts of the garden. It is unfortunate, however, that the whole garden is now divided in three different freeholdings, making it difficult for the modern visitor to appreciate it fully and, above all, making it impossible to implement any single management scheme for the historic landscape as a whole.

Sheffield Park Garden

The Gothic mansion was built before 1779 for the 1st Earl of Sheffield to the designs of James Wyatt. For centuries before, certainly as far back as the 13th century, the estate had intermittently belonged to the de la Warr family. An estate map made under their ownership in 1745 shows that the medieval deer park had by then been turned into a designed landscape with regular plantings of trees, including avenues of oaks and ashes. A little later a lake was created below the house, and an inventory made on Lord de la Warr's death in 1766 lists garden benches and 'a Gothick seat'.

After building his new house Lord Sheffield recruited the services first of Capability Brown and, immediately afterwards, of Humphry Repton. It is very difficult to know exactly what Brown did and where Repton's work starts. Repton later regretted not preparing a 'Red Book' which suggests that he wanted to make clear the extent of his work there. A water-colour by Samuel Hieronymous Grimm of 1787 shows the First Lake (or Ten Foot Pond) with naturalistic plantings of trees by its shores and distant clumps and belts of trees. This would have been too soon for any new plantings by Brown to have made any impact, so presumably this was achieved merely by thinning, and probably de-formalising, existing planting. Repton, who came in 1789 and 1790, later recorded that: 'A very beautiful lake has been added to the scenery of a place which abounds in the most perfect specimens of the picturesque effects produced by Gothic architecture.' Lord Sheffield continued to plant trees in huge quantities until his death in 1822 and, later in the century, his grandson the third Earl commissioned Pulham & Sons to make a cascade and a bridge and to create two more lakes nearer the house. In 1910 the estate was bought by a rich brewer, Arthur Soames, who set about transforming the gardens with formidable energy. In particular

he added immensely to the collection of conifers which the 3rd Earl had started in the latter part of the 19th century. These, despite the losses in the 1987 and 1990 storms, still form the decorative framework of the landscape, especially along the shores of the lakes. Among the evergreens Soames introduced many other ornamental plantings including maples and rhododendrons whose more rounded shapes make a striking contrast with the soaring swamp cypresses (*Taxodium distichum*), *Picea breweriana*, and Western hemlock (*Tsuga heterophylla*) that make such emphatic exclamation marks reflected in the water.

Arthur Soames had no children and his nephew sold the estate in 1953, separating house and garden. The garden passed to the National Trust and is one of the most popular

of all its gardens. It has the character of a landscaped arboretum, with an astonishing range of trees and shrubs, but all visitors, botanists or not, appreciate the exquisite lakeside setting with paths leading off enticingly into the woods. It still preserves the mysterious, dream-like quality which Virginia Woolf noted in 1937 when she described 'The great ponds at Sheffield Place [sic] . . . bordered with red, white and purple reflections, for rhododendrons are massed upon the banks and when the wind passes over the real flowers the water flowers shake and break into each other.'

The Gothic mansion lies in the distance, at the far end of the Middle Lake. Tall conifers make a striking contrast with the mounded shapes of shrubs.

Newby Hall

*S*ome of the best gardens derive their greatest attractions from modern planting with, underlying it, the bones of a much older layout. Newby Hall has features of different periods, but it is the work of the present owners, Robin and Jane Compton, that makes the garden exceptional. The site is an ancient one, recorded as early as the 13th century as being in the ownership of the de Nubie family who gave their name to the place. It was bought in 1689 by Sir William Blackett who shortly afterwards pulled down the old house and built a new one on a site rather further from the river. Legend ascribes its design to Sir Christopher Wren but there is no hard evidence – except for the exceptional beauty of the house itself. In 1748 it was sold to the Weddell family, who added new wings. In 1765, William Weddell met Robert Adam on his Grand Tour and commissioned him to design exquisite new interiors. One of these was a sculpture gallery to house Weddell's newly acquired collection of classical antiquities. All this survives, beautifully restored and cared for by Jane Compton.

The garden history of Newby starts early. By 1694 Sir William Blackett had an excellent head gardener, Peter Aram, a former pupil of the royal gardener George London. Interestingly, Aram was working at Fulham Palace for Bishop Compton, an ancestor of the family today, who recommended him for Newby. Celia Fiennes visited Newby in 1697 and described it as 'the finest house I saw in Yorkshire'. She was no less enthusiastic about the garden, praising 'fine gravel walks . . . borders of flowers and green banks with flower pots'. The Kip engraving made shortly after her visit corroborates her description closely. The picture shows a forecourt with railings to the west of the house from which three avenues radiate, one of which, a double avenue, runs down to the river. Weddell died in 1792 and nothing is known of his gardening activities; by the time Loudon visited in 1837 he found

little to praise – 'A mass of flower beds... extremely ill placed . . . [with] nothing to recommend them and it is seen at a glance that they have no business where they are.' Later in the century the architect William Burges, who built the church at Newby, was probably also responsible for the Statue Walk south of the house. At the turn of the century Ellen Willmott advised on the making of a remarkable rockery and a curved pergola, both of which survive as fine examples of the period.

Today the garden presents a very satisfying mixture of formality and informality. Where in the 18th century there were square plots of grass with statues to the south of the house there is now a superb double mixed herbaceous border – 300 metres long – which forms the main axis to the garden and is backed by hedges of yew running down to the river. The Statue Walk is still in place, forming an emphatic cross axis nearer the house, with billowing Irish yews alternating with statues whose bases are softened by

ABOVE In Sylvia's Garden a Byzantine corn-grinder makes a handsome centrepiece. Flagged paths divide the space in four and the symmetrical plantings and carefully judged colour schemes create a sense of repose.

OPPOSITE A rose pergola leads gently down the hill from the west end of the Statue Walk. It is unusually wide, with bold stone columns and airy iron crosspieces, underplanted with lady's mantle (Alchemilla mollis).

waves of spreading *Cotoneaster horizontalis*. On either side of the herbaceous borders, two pretty gardens of formal design were made in the 1930s: a sunken garden for old-fashioned roses, and an autumn garden. A third, Sylvia's Garden, lies to the north of Statue Walk and is planted as a spring and summer garden. Further from the house, behind the yew hedges that flank the double borders, woodland planting contains an exceptionally rich collection of ornamental trees which includes the National Collection of *Cornus* (dogwoods). Newby is, deservedly, one of the most popular gardens in the north of England.

Westbury Court Garden

Regional variations in English garden styles have in many cases been lost due to the influence of metropolitan taste. The garden at Westbury Court is a genuine oddity, partly because it is of a type unique to the banks of the river Severn downstream from Gloucester. It is rare, too, because the house for which it was made has disappeared and the garden, for long in a derelict state, has survived by the skin of its teeth.

Kip's engraving in Atkyns' *Ancient and Present State of Glostershire* (1712) shows the original Westbury Court garden at its peak. In one corner, near the parish church, is a gabled Jacobean manor house with beyond it a beguiling pattern of alleys, water features and clipped bushes, the whole enclosed in brick walls. At the end of a long, slender canal is a very elegant pillared garden house with a steeply pitched roof.

The estate belonged in the 17th century to the Colchester family and the garden shown in Kip's picture was begun for Maynard Colchester in 1697. One of his neighbours was Catherine Boevey of Flaxted Abbey whose father was an Amsterdam merchant. Her garden, too, had a formal canal, and of the 58 gardens illustrated in Atkyns' book 20 have water gardens. It seems that in the 17th century there was a tradition in this part of England of formal water gardens with a Dutch influence. Westbury is the only surviving example and we know a remarkable amount about its origins from Maynard Colchester's account books which survive in

ABOVE *An early 18th-century figure of Neptune, marooned among the water lilies in the canal.*

OPPOSITE *The parterre, copied from a Kip engraving, is planted entirely with pre-1700 garden plants: dwarf box (Buxus sempervirens 'Suffruticosa'), pot marigold (Calendula officinalis), love-in-the-mist (Nigella damascena) and shrubby candytuft (Iberis sempervirens).*

the Gloucestershire Record Office. These include detailed notes of expenditure on digging canals, the names and quantities of plants, and so on.

The Colchesters remained at Westbury for almost 300 years, during which time two further houses were built and demolished. In 1960 the estate was sold to a developer, and in 1967 the walled garden was acquired by the National Trust who embarked on pioneering restoration. Much of the walls and the essential pattern of the garden had survived, but the garden is prone to flooding from the Severn, and this had resulted in the death of the yew hedges. In their restoration the National Trust were immensely helped by Kip's engraving and the Colchester accounts, and the visitor today may see a garden as close as possible to that which Maynard Colchester had made. The long canal is edged with crisp yew hedges – which, from time to time, break out in lollipops of holly. At the head of the canal the elegant pavilion has been impeccably restored and from its upstairs window the formal gardens are well displayed. Old varieties of fruit trees are trained on the walls – some dating from before Colchester's time – and throughout the garden planting has made use of pre-1700 cultivars. In the main part of the garden, flowers are planted in narrow beds so that their individual qualities may be admired, in true 17th-century fashion. (The deep border with massed planting was a style unknown until the 19th century.) The old atmosphere of the garden has been successfully recaptured and it has regained the character described in *Country Life* in 1908 as being 'dignified and enjoyable, satisfying and alluring'.

Studley Royal

At Studley Royal, walking along the banks of the river Skell as it winds through its exquisite dale, the visitor may follow the evolution of English garden taste in the 18th century. The estate belonged to John Aislabie, of an old Yorkshire family, who inherited it in 1699. A friend of Lord Burlington and of Sir John Vanbrugh, he became Chancellor of the Exchequer in 1718. In 1716 he had started to make a new garden at Studley, quite remote from the house in a beautiful site on the banks of the river which he dammed to make a cascade and laid out immense expanses of formal pools. This gigantic task took about 10 years in all to complete and at times involved 100 labourers. Work was interrupted in 1720 at the time of the South Sea Bubble, when Aislabie was charged with 'a most dangerous and infamous Corruption' and locked up in the Tower of London. He was, however, released in 1723 and retired to his Yorkshire estates to lick his wounds and cultivate his garden. By 1729 he had repaid £2m of his excessive South Sea Company profits; it gives some idea of the wealth that remained to him that not only were his Yorkshire estates untouched but he was able to spend vast sums on his garden and its exquisite buildings *and* leave enough to his son William for him to add substantially to the estate and make another great garden at Hackfall.

After his disgrace Aislabie poured his money and energies into his garden. The first part – the cascade and the geometrical sweeps of water known as the Moon and Crescent Ponds – although formal has none of the rigidity of, say, French and Dutch water gardens of the 17th century. Also, Aislabie's priceless advantage was the uniquely beautiful natural setting of which he took every advantage. The slopes of the valley were planted with beech, elm and Scots pines and the heights were embellished with splendid buildings. These included the banqueting house, almost certainly designed by Colen Campbell, Burlington's protégé, and a Gothic octagonal tower on a rocky eminence above the half-moon lake. A more modest little pavilion, Anne Boleyn's seat, introduces the kind of scenic surprise that 18th-century landscapers relished – the sudden revelation of the ruins of Fountains Abbey on the banks of the river far below. Separated visually from the rest of the garden by a loop of river, this exquisite 12th-century Cistercian abbey had always been envisaged as the ultimate focal point of Aislabie's garden although it did not become part of the estate until long after his death when his son William bought it in 1768.

The formal pools and cascade at Studley Royal do not have the unremitting symmetry of French baroque gardens and their position at the opening of the valley already shows a developing taste for the landscape style. The decorative buildings in commanding positions on the wooded heights belong to the full-blown landscape taste of the mid 18th century. The abbey buildings – surely the ultimate Gothic garden ornament – belong to the later tradition of the picturesque. These different ingredients, however, are successfully bound together by the harmony of their natural setting.

The Temple of Piety reflected in the waters of the Moon Pond with its statue of Neptune, flanked by the Crescent Ponds.

West Dean Gardens

WEST SUSSEX

West Dean Park lies in the valley of the river Lavant, with the West Sussex Downs providing a dramatic backdrop. The house is a vast Gothic mansion designed in 1804 by James Wyatt, not at his most light-hearted. It was substantially altered in 1893 by the architectural firm of George & Peto and the grandiose interiors are of the same date. It is built of the characteristic local building material, flint, which was needed in such vast quantities that local supplies ran out and it had to be imported from elsewhere. The house is now a college teaching a wide range of arts and crafts and is not open to garden visitors.

The earliest garden record goes back to 1622 when James Lewkenor built a house and a park was made at the same time. There is evidence of landscaping dating from 1768 and the park was enlarged in 1804. J. C. Loudon visited in 1829, when Lord Selsey lived here, and was rather dismissive – 'The spot is by no means marked by Nature, and

perhaps something more might have been done by art'. However, he was intrigued by a walk covered in a trellis-work tunnel planted with laburnums and was impressed by the trees, some of which he measured and described for his magisterial eight-volume *Arboretum et Fruticetum Britannicum* (1838). Despite the depredations of the storm in 1987, there are still good trees at West Dean, many planted by visiting royalty and aristocrats during the Edwardian era but some dating back to Loudon's time.

In 1891 William James bought the estate and commissioned new work from George & Peto, and extended the gardens. In the large walled kitchen garden a magnificent range of 13 glasshouses was built for the cultivation of tender fruit and exotic flowers for the house. This garden, recently restored, gives a vivid idea of the garden needs of a prosperous household of the period. Later, in 1911, Harold Peto designed a huge pergola in the grand manner, with fine stone columns and oak cross-pieces, planted with

roses, clematis and wisteria. A stone path runs along the pergola, flanked by bold herbaceous planting. At one end there is a Gothic summerhouse curiously paved with horses' teeth mixed with flint; half way along the pergola the path is interrupted by a formal lily pond. At its far end a thatched summerhouse – on the edge of a well-planted sunken garden – forms an eye-catcher. A separate collection of fine trees and shrubs, St Roche's Arboretum, spreads out on the side of St Roche's hill at some distance from the house.

The garden and park today have a substantially 19th-century character in which specimen trees and touches of formality blend easily. The last member of the family to live here, Edward James, who gave the estate over to an educational charity, was a great patron of the artists of the Surrealistic movement. Alas, no Surrealist took an interest in gardening so, with the exception of two fibreglass trees in the Spring Garden, there is nothing of that influence here.

RIGHT *In the Victorian walled kitchen garden ornamental planting intermingles with vegetables. In this late summer scheme the foliage of a purple form of the castor oil plant (Ricinus communis) associates strikingly with dahlias.*

OPPOSITE *Harold Peto's elaborate pergola seen with a lily pond in the foreground and a Gothic summerhouse at the end. Climbing plants include clematis, roses and wisteria and there is room at the foot of the columns for many herbaceous plants.*

Mottisfont Abbey

*M*ottisfont was an Augustinian foundation dating from the early 13th century built near a spring (*fons*) in the valley of the river Test. At the dissolution of the monasteries the estate passed to Lord Sandys, one of King Henry VIII's courtiers, who exchanged the manors of Chelsea and Paddington for the priory at Mottisfont. The house that Lord Sandys made was almost entirely undone when the estate passed to the Mills family before 1740. The existing house consists of some very attractive 13th-century remains on to which has been grafted an elegant brick house of the George II period. In 1934 the estate was sold to Gilbert Russell whose widow gave it to the National Trust in 1957.

Little is known about the garden at Mottisfont before the 20th century. The fine brick walls of the kitchen garden date from the 1740s when the new house was built. G. F. Prosser in *Select Illustrations of Hampshire* (1833) noticed some good trees – 'the pleasure ground presents some remarkably fine specimens of the plane tree, beech, silver fir, evergreen oak and cypress'. The plane tree referred to is the London plane (*Platanus* × *acerifolia*) which survives and is both exceptionally large and wonderfully beautiful. It is among the two or three largest in the country, although there is some suggestion that it consists of two trees fused together.

Under Gilbert Russell's ownership there were attractive developments in the garden. Extending from the north-west corner of the house a pleached lime walk was designed by Geoffrey Jellicoe in 1936. The trees are planted in little square beds which in the spring are alive with sheets of blue flower-in-the-snow (*Chionodoxa luciliae*) sparkling in the shade. In 1938 Norah Lindsay designed a parterre to lie below the south front of the house. The compartments of box hedging are laid out to echo the design of the fanlight in the front door and bedding plants fill the spaces.

By far the most celebrated feature at Mottisfont is the collection of old roses which was moved to the walled former kitchen garden in the winter of 1972/3. Graham Stuart Thomas, a pioneer among those who rediscovered the old varieties of rose and author of several books on the subject, was also the National Trust's Gardens Adviser. Under his direction the collection was beautifully laid out taking advantage of the splendid walls for climbing varieties and, above all, contriving a setting that makes the collection into a marvellous garden rather than merely a rose museum. He did this by dividing the area, an irregular square, into four areas each edged in box with gravel paths running between them and along the beds that line the walls. It goes without saying that the roses are cultivated with exemplary skill, but gardeners also particularly appreciate the countless ideas for companion planting which Graham Thomas so cleverly provided. This is no snob's tour of rarified planting – white foxgloves or Jacob's ladder, a profusion of multi-coloured columbines, spreading cushions of scented pinks and veils of artemisia or meadow sage provide exactly the right associated plants, unpretentious but effective, among the exquisite roses.

*The rose arbour, of characteristic high Victorian style,
festooned with rambler roses – pale pink 'Debutante'
and purple 'Bleu Magenta'.*

Great Dixter

The particular interest of the gardens at Great Dixter is that their present reputation is substantially the creation of one man, Christopher Lloyd, who is one of the best-known, and influential, garden writers of the day. He is remarkably independent in his views and one of the very few garden writers both trained in horticulture and deeply experienced in the practical aspects of gardening. Visitors to Great Dixter have the pleasure of seeing not some ossified, museum-like garden but one that is in a perpetual state of frequently exhilarating evolution.

The house at Great Dixter is a 15th-century hall house most beautifully extended

The bold purple foliage of Canna indica *'Purpurea' makes a striking background to dahlia 'Bishop of Llandaff' and the airy flower heads of* Verbena bonariensis.

in 1910 under the direction of Sir Edwin Lutyens for Christopher Lloyd's father Nathaniel, himself an architect and the author of an excellent book on yew and box in the garden. Lutyens also had a hand in laying out the gardens with yew hedges and Nathaniel Lloyd himself added decorative topiary and designed a handsome sunken garden in a yard between barns with fastidious regard for masonry and brickwork. Christopher Lloyd

was brought up here and, after training and subsequently lecturing in horticulture, returned in 1954 and gradually imposed his firm stamp on the character of the place.

The most celebrated scene of his gardening experiments has been the famous Long Border. It lies at the east end of the house, facing south-west, 60 metres long and 4.5 metres deep, edged with a path of stone flags. Lloyd was a pioneer of the mixed border, the subject of his first book (*The Mixed Border*, 1957) and many articles, in which *all* kinds of plants are encouraged to cohabit in close-packed promiscuity. This extends, of course, to both woody and perennial herbaceous plants but also to tender bedding plants which

can be planted in early summer when permanent planting is beginning to flag. Lloyd's Long Border has an exceptionally long season of interest – from April to October and beyond. It is a distinctly modern style of gardening; in the gardens of a previous generation, if the rose garden, for example, was past its prime one would simply move to a different part of the garden and look at something else. The Long Border, although much bigger than most gardeners will manage, is thus a model way of planting for the smaller garden where long periods of interest are essential.

Lloyd is very impatient with excessively fastidious 'good taste' in colour associations,

Scarlet pokers, cerise and purple phlox and parti-coloured dahlias stand out against a background of the sombre foliage of Cotinus coggygria *with the yellow flowers of a soaring verbascum giving an unexpected but pleasing jolt.*

and regular visitors to his Long Border will find some highly personal juxtapositions which, at the very least, will never be dull. It would be entirely wrong to think of him, however, as a hopeless colour addict for he has always placed great emphasis on leaf form as an essential part of the gardener's art. His book *Foliage Plants* (1973) is a brilliant endorsement of that side of a plant's character and the Long Border shows the principles in

action. Here such plants as cardoon, the holly *Ilex* 'Golden King', *Euonymus* × *fortunei* 'Silver Queen', *Helleborus foetidus*, the graceful grass *Miscanthus sinensis* 'Silver Feather', and the beautiful golden cut-leafed elder *Sambucus racemosa* 'Plumosa Aurea' show the decorative potential of foliage alone.

Christopher Lloyd's most influential book has been *The Well-Tempered Garden* (1970) which gives a comprehensive view of the art and practice of his style of gardening. It is very much more than a recipe book, offering the reader, apart from a wealth of practical help, a way of looking at plants and gardens which will encourage experimentation and a wariness of shop-worn conventions in garden taste.

Holdenby House

Old gardens are often of such powerful character that, although most of the detail and all the planting may disappear, a vivid atmosphere of the past may survive. Holdenby House was one of the great Renaissance palaces of England and, under Sir Christopher Hatton, had one of the greatest gardens. Hatton was a remarkable figure. He was Lord Chancellor to Queen Elizabeth I and an intimate of hers. So intimate, indeed, that he was rumoured to be her lover. He was at the very least a loyal and effective royal servant and was rewarded with vast estates to add to the Hatton property of Holdenby. One of these was Ely Palace in London from which the Bishop of Ely was evicted by the Queen to provide a town house for her Lord Chancellor. He gardened in both places and his London activities are commemorated in the street name Hatton Garden.

The palace at Holdenby was built between 1570 and 1583 under the influence of Italian architectural theorists of the Italian Renaissance such as Alberti and Serlio whose books had been published in English. They believed that the garden should be in harmony with the house – a novel idea in England at the time. At Holdenby an immense platform of earth jutted out from the centre of the house with an elaborate patchwork of parterres. On each side terraces descended, with a pond on one side and a bowling alley on the other. These terraces still survive, plainly visible on the ground, and the broad layout may be discerned in aerial photographs.

In the Civil War, Holdenby was taken over by the Parliamentarians, who imprisoned Charles I here in 1647. After his execution the house was sold and then demolished except for the kitchen wing. This formed the basis of the present house which was added to in the 19th century. A pair of magnificent stone and brick gateways dated 1583 survive, now marooned in a field, with the eastern terraces visible below them. These

gateways originally led into an entrance courtyard to one side of the house. In the making of his garden Sir Christopher Hatton ordered the demolition of a village which he then rebuilt on a symmetrical plan positioned, in true renaissance spirit, on the axis of the new garden. A surviving drawing, made just after the completion of the gardens, shows this in great detail, including the pattern of a vast parterre.

Holdenby is well worth visiting today – the sculpted land and ornamental gateways that lead nowhere create a memorable impression. It is well cared for by the present owners who commissioned Rosemary Verey in 1980 to design a new miniature formal garden in the Elizabethan spirit. She enclosed it in hedges of yew, giving it the character of a secret garden, and restricted her layout to those plants available in English gardens by 1580. A pattern of shapes of clipped box follows a path encircling a sundial and the surrounding beds are rich with the scent of artemisia, balm, hyssop, lavender and rue. It makes a charming link with the great Elizabethan garden that was lost.

LEFT *One of the surviving great arches, dated 1583, which were part of Sir Christopher Hatton's grandiose late Tudor garden.*

RIGHT *Mounds of santolina, topiary shapes of box and billowing bushes of rosemary give decorative structure to the Tudor garden designed by Rosemary Verey. A shady summerhouse is fashioned of clipped yew.*

Badminton House

AVON

The estate at Badminton was acquired in 1608 by Edward Somerset, 4th Earl of Worcester, then living at Raglan Castle in Monmouthshire. It did not become the family's chief residence until after the Restoration when the old house was rebuilt and at some time in the late 17th century a grandiose new garden was laid out. In 1682 the 3rd Marquis of Worcester had been created 1st Duke of Beaufort and was in need of an estate of appropriately ducal splendour. Paintings, drawings and engravings from this period give a vivid impression of the scale of the work. A drawing of c.1670 by Hendrik Danckerts shows the newly rebuilt house from the north with parkland and a sketchy avenue extending away from the house. By 1699 Leonard Knyff had been to paint views of the estate and Kip's engravings of them show one of the most spectacular gardens of its time. A general view displays the house at the centre of a vast pattern of radiating avenues, criss-crossing the land, with parks allocated to different kinds of deer (red deer, fallow deer, 'Virginia' deer). Detailed views of the area about the house depict bewilderingly elaborate formal gardens with a chief axis running east of the house passing between ornate parterres and piercing a huge formal wilderness of hedges. Two paintings by Thomas Smith of c.1705, still at Badminton House, corroborate the general evidence of these pictures although they contradict it in details.

The late 17th-century formal gardens were not to last long. By the time Canaletto painted his two famous views of the house and park in 1748 a very different atmosphere prevailed, with little trace of grand formality. The intriguing figure of Thomas Wright, 'the wizard of Durham', had already been at work. Although his scheme for the east front with winding paths, a menagerie, a 'magical' mathematical grove and other wonders was never executed, he built a rustic hermitage in 1747, one of only two 18th-century her-

mitages to survive in England. A Root House (with a framework of contorted roots), 'ragged castle' and an eye-catcher, 'Castle Barn', were also built to his designs. A little earlier William Kent had been called in to work on the house. In the park, in about 1745, he built the exquisite Worcester Lodge on the brow of a hill to terminate an avenue three kilometres from the north front of the house. This domed building, flanked by lodges crowned with pyramids, has a beautiful upstairs dining room where meals were taken and distant views of the house admired.

Traces of the late 17th-century avenues still survive at Badminton. But the story of the garden is by no means all in the past. The late Duchess of Beaufort was an expert gardener. As Lady Caroline Somerset she commissioned, from 1964 onwards, brilliant designs from Russell Page for the Dower House at Badminton. Subsequently Page was asked to design a new formal garden on the historic site east of the house where he laid out a characteristically restrained but effective pattern of yew and box – his last commission.

ABOVE *From the arch of Worcester Lodge the ground slopes southwards towards the house. An avenue three kilometres long links house and lodge.*

RIGHT *William Kent's Worcester Lodge rises on the brow of a hill, making a delicious eye-catcher from several viewpoints.*

Sissinghurst Castle

KENT

'*Never* has Sissinghurst looked more lovely,' wrote Harold Nicolson to his wife Vita Sackville-West in 1937, '...you with your extraordinary taste have made it look like nobody's garden but your own.' The name 'Sissinghurst' has assumed the dimensions of a myth, denoting a whole way of gardening but also, because of the wildly unconventional behaviour of its owners, a way of life. Although on the whole this has had a distorting effect on our view of the garden at Sissinghurst, nevertheless its story is inescapably that of Vita Sackville-West. She was a rare mixture of sense and sensibility. A poet, with a rich imaginative life, she was also a profoundly knowledgeable, practical gardener. Her writings about gardening, in particular the weekly column she wrote for the *Observer* from 1947 to 1961, are among the best 20th-century garden literature. They show a gardener intimately in touch with her subject in a practical way but at the same time deeply responsive to the poetry and aesthetics of plants and gardens.

Vita Sackville-West was born at Knole and that great house and its history gave powerful inspiration to her creativity. She married Harold Nicolson in 1913 and they spent their early married life in Constantinople where Harold was posted as a diplomat. They lived, as she wrote, in 'a wooden Turkish house, with a little garden and a pergola of grapes and a pomegranate tree covered with scarlet fruit'. In 1915 they bought a house called Long Barn, not far from Knole, where she made her first garden.

In 1930 they bought Sissinghurst Castle – a jumble of wildly romantic, mostly Tudor buildings in a ruinous state with a garden filled with rubbish 'muddled up in a tangle of bindweed, nettles and ground elder'. This, when the ground was cleared, provided a marvellous sequence of spaces, with beautiful walls and decorative buildings, in which to make a garden. They worked in partnership, with Harold largely responsible for the overall pattern and Vita for the detailed planting. Her taste for the abundant and dramatic was tempered by his love of classical order and discipline. Her taste in plants ranged widely, from a love of roses – of which Sissinghurst had a pioneer collection and which still provides a major theme – to the simplicity of old apple trees. She would combine the two extremes – with the aristocratic old Alba rose 'Madame Plantier' trained into an apple tree in the orchard. But she was no plant snob – she was perfectly capable of writing an article 'In defence of the lobelia'.

Sissinghurst became a garden of compartments, affording varied settings for different styles of planting and strikingly contrasting effects. A cool green corridor of yew runs along the east side of the richly planted formal enclosures, separating them from an orchard beyond. A white garden, with an intricate pattern of box-edged beds, has a mysteriously Moorish air. A rondel of yew hedges provides a calm centre to a vast expanse of old roses. The south cottage has a garden of brilliant oranges and reds – 'a muddle of flowers, but all of them in the range of colours you might find in a sunset'.

Vita Sackville-West died in 1962 and Nicolson in 1968. They left Sissinghurst to the National Trust which inherited two outstanding gardeners who had worked with Vita Sackville-West – Pamela Schwerdt and Sibylle Kreutzberger, who carried on the tradition she had established. They have now retired and Sarah Cook is in charge. Gardens maintained as shrines are without life; Sissinghurst has changed in the last 30 years and remains an exquisitely beautiful garden. It is, perhaps, the greatest success of its original makers that they devised a plan and a style of gardening that may be reinterpreted and given life long after their deaths.

Spring in the nuttery with its Kentish cob-nuts and dense underplanting of ferns, geraniums, spurges and woodruff.

Tresco Abbey

The key to the gardens at Tresco is the remarkable climate it enjoys. Here in the Scilly Isles, far south-west of the tip of the Cornish mainland, frosts are rare, hours of sunshine are long and the encircling sea gives high levels of humidity. The only obstacles to gardening are the fierce winds to which all westerly parts of the Britain are subjected. The Benedictines came to Tresco in the 10th century but before the dissolution of the monasteries the abbey had fallen into disrepair.

The garden history of the island begins in 1834 when Augustus Smith came to live on Tresco. He built a new house and immediately embarked on the making of the garden. There were no trees when he started,

famous. Augustus died in 1872 and was succeeded by his nephew Algernon Smith Dorrien Smith who changed his surname to Dorrien-Smith. Subsequent generations of Dorrien-Smiths have made their contributions to the gardens but their essential character, and indeed their extent, have not changed since the days of Augustus Smith.

The gardens lie on the south-western tip of the island and slope southwards, sometimes quite sharply. Although they are densely planted, in places convincingly evoking a sub-tropical jungle, the layout has been skilfully designed. A series of walks, either following the contours of the slopes or plummeting straight downwards, impose a

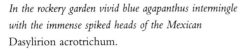

In the rockery garden vivid blue agapanthus intermingle with the immense spiked heads of the Mexican Dasylirion acrotrichum.

and the planting of windbreaks was an essential priority. He terraced the precipitous slopes and quite early on began to introduce the tender plants, for example a collection of succulents, that have made the garden

pattern and open piercing views through the foliage. Tresco is one of the finest plant treasuries in the world, but it is quite wrong to think of it in merely botanical terms.

In many departments it has the most comprehensive collection of any British garden. Indeed in the whole of Europe only one or two Mediterranean gardens, such as the Giardino Hanbury at La Mortola, can

rival it. Plants of the southern hemisphere, especially of Australasia, are particularly well represented. Many of these are shrubs – almost 50 species and cultivars of olearia and a much greater number of hebes, for example – but many are full-blown trees such as eucalyptus (at least 20 species) and acacia. Everywhere there are tender herbaceous plants, some of which, such as *Geranium*

maderense and *Echium pininana*, self-seed prolifically and are found all over the garden. Of especial interest to gardeners from the cold mainland are the many kinds of pelargonium that grow out of doors. Some of these are familiar cultivars but there are also the much more rarely seen species.

In 1987 Tresco suffered from catastrophically cold weather which destroyed immense numbers of plants. In 1990 further damage was done when storms laid waste much of the surrounding shelter belts that protect tender plants from strong, salty sea winds. Restoration has been achieved with remarkable speed, aided by the English Heritage grants scheme, and once again this unique garden presents an appearance of marvellous abundance and variety.

The rocky slopes are planted with a bewildering profusion of exotics looking very much at home. Agaves contribute bold leaf form and there are lively colours from pelargoniums, blue and white agapanthus and red sedums. Such apparently artless arrangements demand high standards of maintenance.

Heale Gardens

In the well-watered Woodford Valley, Heale House lies right on the bank of the river Avon in a secluded position, invisible from the road. An avenue of beech trees lines the drive and the house is only glimpsed at the last moment, half-concealed by trees. Built in the 17th century, of a characteristic Wiltshire mixture of fine brick and stone dressings, it was enlarged towards the end of the 19th century by the Arts and Crafts architect Detmar Blow whose work is scarcely distinguishable from the original. It is an immensely decorative house which is given its full ornamental value by the gardens that surround it.

The estate was bought in 1890 by the Hon. Louis Greville who commissioned Harold Peto to make designs for the gardens in 1906. Peto, an architect and son of Sir Morton Peto of Somerleyton Hall, had opened an office in Nice in 1892 from which he designed many Riviera houses and gardens. His gardens were of a markedly architectural kind, inspired by the precepts of Italian Renaissance gardens and imbued with a love of classical discipline. In England, especially in the south-west, he designed

ABOVE *Balustrades by the river terrace are garlanded with roses, some of which are unique to the garden. On the left is the bold foliage of* Gunnera manicata.

OPPOSITE *The formal gardens in front of the south front of the house were designed by Harold Peto, and are arranged around a long central axis whose focal point is a pair of wrought-iron gates leading into a field.*

several gardens of architectural character which slip unobtrusively into the rural landscape. At Heale his chief work was the West Garden, a symmetrical terraced garden, aligned on the front door of the house, rising gently to a paved cross terrace on the top level. The planting here is almost entirely the work of Mr Greville's great-niece, Lady Anne Rasch, who came here in 1959. She replaced Peto's labour-intensive herbaceous scheme with one of mixed shrubs and perennials, many old roses and repeated plantings of such decorative shrubs as *Cotinus coggygria* 'Royal Purple' and the golden-leafed *Philadelphus coronarius* 'Aureus'.

In 1901, Mr Greville, a former diplomat in Tokyo, began a Japanese garden south of the house, with a tea-house suspended above the

water, snow lanterns and a brilliant scarlet arched bridge looking completely at home among willows. Across a lawn is the 18th-century former kitchen garden, enclosed in traditional cob walls, and now planted with fruit, vegetables and ornamental plants. A pergola, built in 1968, runs along the south side, edged with box hedges and festooned with the voluptuous rose 'Easlea's Golden Rambler' and the purple-leafed vine *Vitis vinifera* 'Purpurea'. Tunnels of espaliered apple trees divide the garden down the middle with a pool at the centre surrounded by box clipped into giant mounds. Beds running along the walls are filled with ornamental planting and central beds are devoted to fruit, vegetables and cutting flowers.

The garden at Heale House is an excellent example of a peculiarly English type whose distinctive quality is to yoke together very different ingredients into a harmonious unity. The wonderfully decorative old house by the banks of the winding river, Peto's terraces, the exotic Japanese Garden, the mixture of ornamental plants with fruit and vegetables in the walled garden – all seem inevitable, as though part of some unvoiced master plan.

Belsay Hall

In spring the brilliant colours of rhododendron flowers make a striking contrast with the raw stone surfaces of the ravine.

Belsay Hall is an austere Greek Revival mansion built between 1810 and 1817 and made slightly less chilly in appearance by the warm honey-coloured local stone. It was designed by its owner, Sir Charles Monck, who had changed his name from Middleton to inherit from his mother's family. He was inspired by the classical Greek architecture which he had studied on his honeymoon during which he spent a year in Athens. The stone for the hall was quarried on the site and the resulting ravine was transformed by Sir Charles into a unique landscape inspired by theories of the Picturesque. The Picturesque was a reaction to what was seen as the blandness of the landscapes of Capability Brown with their smooth uneventful turf and rounded clumps of trees. It sought something much rougher, more exciting and, above all, dramatic. The great philosopher of the Picturesque was the Herefordshire squire, collector, poet and dilettante Richard Payne Knight. In his poem *The Landscape* (1794) he ridiculed the insipidity of Brown and mocked Humphry Repton's 'prim gravel walks, through which we winding go,/in endless serpentines that nothing show'.

The Middletons had lived at Belsay since the 14th century when they built Belsay Castle which still survives, picturesquely dishevelled, as the culmination of the chief garden walk. The Buck brothers' engraving of the castle of 1728 shows a formal walled garden laid out in front of the castle, entirely typical of its period, with symmetrical rows of alternating spherical and pyramidal shrubs, and statues gazing across lawns. In the second

The planting in the quarry garden, although exotic, is naturalistically arranged and takes advantage of the different habitats provided. Many shade-loving plants, especially ferns, flourish here but the ravine also provides protection for quite tender plants such as the Japanese anglica tree Aralia elata.

half of the 18th century there was much planting in the newly landscaped parkland, and Castle Bantam, a fashionable Gothic *ferme ornée*, was built by Sir William Middleton.

Sir Charles Monck's Quarry Garden makes a striking contrast to the atmosphere of his new hall. A path winds uphill flanked by the craggy, vertiginous walls of rough-hewn rock whose height Sir Charles emphasised by planting yew trees at their crest. The planting of the ravine was an interesting example of pioneer naturalistic planting, choosing plants appropriate for the ecology. By 1854, for example, 28 species of fern (many of which

may still be seen) had been introduced. Sir Charles' grandson, Sir Arthur Middleton, added more exotic flowering shrubs to the Quarry Garden such as rhododendrons, which in flower give a vivid impression of some Himalayan ravine. The path eventually emerges into pasture land with the remains of

the castle forming a marvellous eye-catcher, rising up among the long grass. To emerge from the shade and damp of the ravine into the open space of the meadow is exhilarating.

The floriferous south-facing terraces are contemporary with the house and there are interesting later additions. Sir Arthur made a novel labour-saving 'winter garden' of close-planted heathers and introduced many ornamental trees and shrubs, including some fine magnolias. But it is the unique Quarry Garden that is the great feature of Belsay, important in garden history and enchanting to garden visitors.

Birmingham Botanical Gardens

It is a little misleading to refer to these gardens as 'botanical' because their primary character is that of a public park. They were created by the Birmingham Botanical and Horticultural Society which was founded in 1829 and acquired the site in

futuristic design shaped like a giant beehive with an immense spiral central staircase from which visitors could look down on a jungle of tropical vegetation below. Had it been built it would have been the largest of its time – predating Paxton's Crystal Palace by 20 years.

summer months. The Victorian atmosphere is very well preserved, with virtuoso displays of summer bedding plants, but a distinguished and immensely varied collection of plants is still maintained here.

The great plant hunter E. H. 'China'

RIGHT *The bold ornamental foliage of* Strelitzia augusta *hangs down over a pool in the tropical house.*

OPPOSITE *In the glasshouses an immense range of tropical and sub-tropical plants is grown. A date palm* (Phoenix dactylifera) *and the fleshy leaves of a banana* (Musa × paradisaica) *are visible behind the fountain.*

1831. John Claudius Loudon, then at the height of his fame, was asked to design new gardens for the sloping 16-acre site and he laid out a characteristically fluent design with the various levels linked by winding walks. It was unfortunate that Loudon's entire scheme was never executed, for it included a spectacular circular glasshouse on the site of the present range of glasshouses. It was a

The gardens grew quickly, opening to the public in 1832 and by 1834 displaying no fewer than 9,000 species of plants, and they continued to flourish throughout the 19th century. Today they combine an excellent collection of plants, display gardens to give gardeners ideas for layouts, and a public garden – including a bandstand where a band plays every Sunday afternoon during the

Wilson, who worked here from 1893 to 1897, was one of the most prolific discoverers of new plants, especially in China, and a collection of plants introduced by him has been gathered together in his honour. It includes entirely familiar things such as the regal lily (*Lilium regale*), the witch hazel (*Hamamelis mollis*), the universal cottage-garden hedging plant *Lonicera nitida*, as well as

the much less common and very beautiful 'pocket handkerchief tree', *Davidia involucrata*.

Glasshouses were an essential part of every great 19th-century garden and in public gardens they had the particular purpose of displaying exotic plants from the remote corners of the Empire. Birmingham still maintains a range of glasshouses with a tropical collection, palms and succulents. The late 19th-

century craze for climbing, particularly in the Alps, stimulated a fashion for rock, or Alpine, gardens; William Robinson's *Alpine Flowers for Gardens*, the first book on the subject, was published in 1871. The rock garden at Birmingham was made between 1894 and 1895 by the specialist firm of James Backhouse & Sons of York who brought down over 100 tonnes of millstone grit boulders. Today Alpine

phlox, campanulas, gentians and saxifrages flourish in a scree garden.

Birmingham Botanical Gardens present a lively scene, thronged with visitors of all kinds. Its 19th-century atmosphere has been successfully maintained and it continues to fulfil the idealistic aims of its founders – to provide an attractive place of leisure and education.

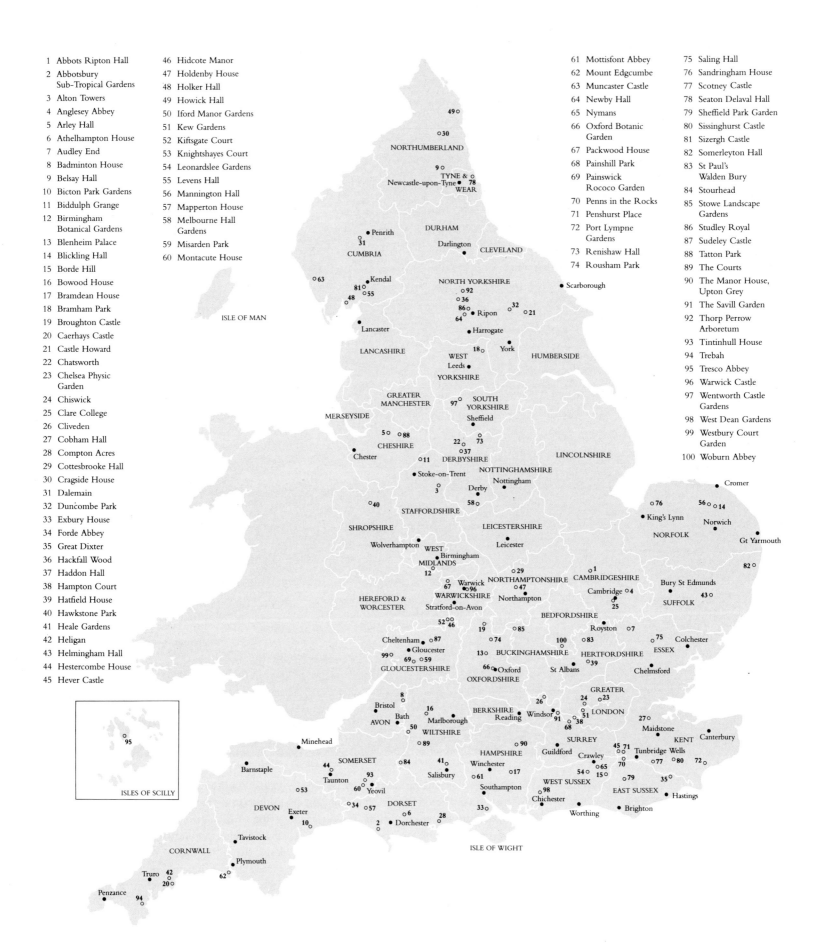

Avon

BADMINTON HOUSE
GL9 1DB
Tel: 01454 218 346 for opening times.

Bedfordshire

WOBURN ABBEY
MK43 0TP
Tel: 01525 290666
Opening times: end December-end March weekends 10.30-3.45; end March-end October daily 10-4.30. The private gardens have limited openings and guided tours only.

Berkshire

CLIVEDEN
Taplow, Maidenhead, SL6 0JA
Tel: 01628 605069
Opening times: daily March-September 11-6; October-December 11-4

Buckinghamshire

STOWE LANDSCAPE GARDENS
Buckingham, MK18 5EH
Tel: 01280 822850
Opening times: Monday, Wednesday, Friday and Sunday 10-5

Cambridgeshire

ABBOTS RIPTON HALL
Huntingdon, PE17 2PQ
Tel: 01487 7735655 for opening times.

ANGLESEY ABBEY
Lode, Cambridge, CB5 9EJ
Tel: 01223 811200 for opening times.

CLARE COLLEGE
Trinity Lane, Cambridge, CB2 1TL
Tel: 01223 333200
Opening times: Monday to Friday throughout the year 2-4, and some weekends in July, August and September.

Cheshire

ARLEY HALL
Near Northwich, CW9 6NA
Tel: 01565 777353
Opening times: April-October, Tuesday to Sunday and Bank Holiday Mondays 12-5

TATTON PARK
Knutsford, WA16 6QN
Tel: 01565 654822
Opening times: daily April-September 10.30-5; October-March 11-3

Cornwall

CAERHAYS CASTLE
Gorran, St Austell, PL26 6LY
Tel: 01872 501144
Opening times: end March-early May, Monday to Friday 11-4.30

THE LOST GARDENS OF HELIGAN
Nr Mevagissey, St Austell, PL26 6EN
Tel: 01726 844157 or 843566
Opening times: daily 10-4.30 (last admission)

MOUNT EDGCUMBE
Cremyll, Torpoint, PL10 1HZ
Tel: 01752 822236
Opening times: park and lower gardens daily 8 to dusk; Earl's Garden and House 11-5 Wednesday to Sunday and Bank Holidays, April-October

TREBAH
Mawnan Smith, Nr Falmouth, TR11 5JZ
Tel: 01326 250448
Opening times: daily 10.30-5 (last admission)

Cumbria

DALEMAIN
Penrith, CA10 0HB
Tel: 017684 86450
Opening times: April-October, Sunday to Thursday 11.15-5

HOLKER HALL
Cark-In-Cartmel, Grange-over-Sands, LA11 7PL
Tel: 015395 58328
Opening times: April-October, Sunday to Friday 10-6 (last admission 4.30)

LEVENS HALL
Kendal, LA8 0PD
Tel: 015395 60321
Opening times: April-September, Sunday to Thursday 11-5

MUNCASTER CASTLE
Ravenglass, CA18 1RQ
Tel: 01229 717614
Opening times: daily 11-5

SIZERGH CASTLE
Nr Kendal, LA8 8AE
Tel: 015395 60070
Opening times: Sunday to Thursday 12.30-5.30

Derbyshire

CHATSWORTH
Bakewell, DE45 1PP
Tel: 01246 582204
Opening times: late March-October daily 11-5 (last admission)

HADDON HALL
Bakewell, DE45 1LA
Tel: 01629 812855
Opening times: April-September 11-5.45 (last admission 5); closed Sundays in July and August

MELBOURNE HALL GARDENS
Melbourne, DE73 1EN
Tel: 01332 862502
Opening times: April-September 2-6 Wednesday, Saturday, Sunday and Bank Holidays

RENISHAW HALL
Renishaw, Sheffield, S31 9WB
Tel: 01246 432042 for opening times.

Devonshire

BICTON PARK GARDENS
East Budleigh, Budleigh Salterton, EX9 7DP
Tel: 01395 568 465
Opening times: daily April-September 10-6; March and October 10-4

KNIGHTSHAYES COURT
Tiverton, EX16 7RQ
Tel: 01884 257381
Opening times: April-October daily 11-5.30

Dorset

ABBOTSBURY SUB-TROPICAL GARDENS
Abbotsbury, Weymouth, DT3 4LA
Tel: 01305 871387
Opening times: daily summer 10-5; winter 10 to dusk

ATHELHAMPTON HOUSE
Athelhampton, Dorchester, DT2 7LG
Tel: 01305 848363
Opening times: April-October, Tuesday, Wednesday, Thursday, Sunday and Bank Holidays 12-5; July-August, Monday and Friday 12-5

COMPTON ACRES
Canford Cliffs Road, Poole, BH13 7ES
Tel: 01202 700778
Opening times: daily 10.30-6.30

FORDE ABBEY
Nr Chard, TA20 4LU
Tel: 01460 220231
Opening times: daily 10-4.30; House 1-4.30 Sunday, Wednesday and Bank Holidays

MAPPERTON HOUSE
Nr Beaminster, DT8 3NR
Tel: 01308 862645
Opening times: March-October daily 2-6

East Sussex

GREAT DIXTER
Northiam, Rye, TN31 6PH
Tel: 01797 252878
Opening times: April-mid-October, Tuesday to Sunday 2-5 (and Bank Holidays)

PENNS IN THE ROCKS
Groombridge, Tunbridge Wells, TN3 9PA
Tel: 01892 864244 for opening times.

SHEFFIELD PARK GARDEN
Sheffield Park, Uckfield, TN22 3QX
Tel: 01825 790231 for opening times.

Essex

AUDLEY END
Saffron Walden
Tel: 01799 522399
Opening times: Wednesday to Sunday (and Bank Holidays) 10-5; House 12-5

SALING HALL
Great Saling, Nr Braintree, CM7 5DT
Tel: 01371 850243
Opening times: May-July, Wednesday 2-5

Gloucestershire

HIDCOTE MANOR
Hidcot Bartrim, Chipping Campden, GL55 6LR
Tel: 01386 43833
Opening times: April-October daily, except Tuesday and Friday, 11-6

KIFTSGATE COURT
Chipping Campden, GL55 6LW
Tel: 01386 438777
Opening times: April-September, Wednesday, Thursday and Sunday 2-6; Saturdays in June and July, and Bank Holidays, 2-6

MISARDEN PARK
Stroud, GL6 7JA
Tel: 01285 821303
Opening times: Easter-end September, Tuesday, Wednesday and Thursday 9.30-4.30

PAINSWICK ROCOCO GARDEN
Painswick House, Painswick, GL6 6TH
Tel: 01452 813204
Opening times: Wednesday to Sunday 11-5

SUDELEY CASTLE
Winchcombe, Cheltenham, GL54 5JD
Tel: 01242 604357
Opening times: daily March 11-4; April-October 10.30-5.30

WESTBURY COURT GARDEN
Westbury-on-Severn, GL14 1PD
Tel: 01452 760461
Opening times: April-end October, Wednesday to Sunday and Bank Holidays 11-6 (closed Good Friday); other months by appointment

Greater London

CHELSEA PHYSIC GARDEN
66 Royal Hospital Road, SW3 4HS
Tel: 0171 353 5646
Opening times: April-October, Wednesday 2-5 and Sunday 2-6

CHISWICK HOUSE
Burlington Lane, W4 2RP
Tel: 0181 995 0508
Opening times: daily 7.30 to dusk

Hampshire

BRAMDEAN HOUSE
Nr Alresford, SO24 0JU
Tel: 01962 771214 for opening times.

EXBURY HOUSE
Exbury, Southampton, SO45 1AZ
Tel: 01703 891203
Opening times: mid-February-late October daily 10-5.30 (or dusk if earlier)

THE MANOR HOUSE
Upton Grey, Basingstoke, RG25 2RD
Tel: 01256 862827
Opening times: May-July, Wednesday 2-4.30. Groups by appointment.

MOTTISFONT ABBEY
Romsey, SO51 0LP
Tel: 01794 341220 or 340757
Opening times: April-May and July-October, Saturday to Wednesday 12-6; June, Saturday to Thursday 12-8.30

Hertfordshire

HATFIELD HOUSE
Hatfield, AL9 5NQ
Tel: 01707 262823
Opening times: West Gardens: end March-early October, daily 11-6 (closed Good Friday); East Gardens: Monday 2-5 (closed Bank Holidays)

ST PAUL'S WALDEN BURY
St Paul's Walden, Hitchin, SG4 8DP
Tel: 01438 871218 for opening times.

Isles of Scilly

TRESCO ABBEY
Isles of Scilly, TR24 0QQ
Tel: 01720 422849
Opening times: daily 10-4

Kent

COBHAM HALL
Cobham, DA12 3BL
Tel: 01474 824319 or 823371
Opening times: April, July and August, most Wednesdays, Thursdays and Sundays 2-5 (last admission 4.45)

HEVER CASTLE
Nr Edenbridge, TN8 7NG
Tel: 01732 865224
Opening times: daily March to November 11 to dusk

PENSHURST PLACE
Penshurst, Tonbridge, TN11 8DG
Tel: 01892 870307
Opening times: April-October and weekends in March, 11-6

PORT LYMPNE GARDENS
Port Lympne Estates, Lympne, CT21 4PD
Tel: 01303 264647
Opening times: 10 to dusk daily, except Christmas

SCOTNEY CASTLE
Lamberhurst, TN3 8JN
Tel: 01892 891081
Opening times: April-end October,
Wednesday to Friday 11-6, Saturday
and Sunday 2-6 or dusk if earlier;
Bank Holidays 12-6; closed Good
Friday. (Last admission 1hr
before closing.)

SISSINGHURST CASTLE
Sissinghurst, Nr Cranbrook,
TN17 2AB
Tel: 01580 712850
Opening times: April-October,
Tuesday to Friday 1-6.30, Saturday,
Sunday and Good Friday 10-5.30.
(Last admission ½ hr before closing.)

Norfolk

BLICKLING HALL
Blickling, Norwich, NR11 6NF
Tel: 01263 733084
Opening times: March-October,
Tuesday, Wednesday, Friday to
Sunday and Bank Holidays 11-5

MANNINGTON HALL
Norwich, NR11 7BB
Tel: 0126 3584175
Opening times: Easter-October,
Sunday 12-5; June-August,
Wednesday, Thursday and
Friday 11-5

SANDRINGHAM HOUSE
Sandringham, PE35 6EN
Tel: 01553 772675
Opening times: Easter-October
10.30-4.45. Closed two weeks
around end of July – call for details.

Northamptonshire

COTTESBROOKE HALL
Cottesbrooke, NN6 8PF
Tel: 01604 505808
Opening times: end April-end
September, Thursday 2-5.30. Bank
Holidays 2-5.30. (Last admission 5.)

HOLDENBY HOUSE
Holdenby, NN6 8OJ
Tel: 01604 770074
Opening times: Easter-end September,
Sunday 2-6; July-August, Thursday
1-5; Bank Holidays 1-6

Northumberland

BELSAY HALL
Belsay, Nr Ponteland, NE20 0DX
Tel: 01661 881636
Opening times: daily April-October
10-6; November-March 10-4

CRAGSIDE HOUSE
Rothbury, Morpeth, NE65 7PX
Tel: 01669 620333 or 620266
Opening times: daily April-October
10.30-5.30; Country Park 10.30-7;
House 1-5.30

HOWICK HALL
Nr Alnwick, NE66 3LB
Tel: 01665 577285
Opening times: daily April-
October 1-6

SEATON DELAVAL HALL
Seaton Sluice, Whitley Bay,
NE26 4QR
Tel: 0191 2373040 or 1493
Opening times: May-September,
Wednesday, Sunday and Bank
Holidays 2-6

North Yorkshire

CASTLE HOWARD
York, YO6 7DA
Tel: 01653 648333
Opening times: mid-March-late
October 10 to dusk.
(Last admission 4.30.)

DUNCOMBE PARK
Helmsley, YO6 5EB
Tel: 01439 770213
Opening times: 11-4.30. July-
August, daily; May, June and
September, Wednesday to Saturday;
April and October, Wednesday
and Sunday

HACKFALL WOOD
Grewelthorpe, Nr Ripon
Opening times: daily from dawn
to dusk

NEWBY HALL
Ripon, HG4 5AE
Tel: 01423 322583
Opening times: April-September,
Tuesday to Sunday 11-5.30; House
12-5.00

STUDLEY ROYAL
Fountains Abbey and
Studley Royal
Ripon, HG4 3DY
Tel: 01765 608888 or 601005
Opening times: January-March 10-5
(or dusk if earlier); April-September
10-7; October-December 10-5 (or
dusk if earlier). Closed Fridays during
November, December and January.

**THORP PERROW
ARBORETUM**
Bedale, DL8 2PR
Tel: 01677 425323
Opening times: daily from dawn
to dusk

Oxfordshire

BLENHEIM PALACE
Woodstock, OX20 1PX
Tel: 01993 811325
Opening times: daily mid-March-end
October, 10.30-4.45

BROUGHTON CASTLE
Banbury, OX15 5EB
Tel: 01295 262624 or 720041
Opening times: 2-5, mid-May-mid-
September, Wednesday and Sunday;
July and August, Thursday;
Bank Holidays

**OXFORD BOTANIC
GARDEN**
Rose Lane, Oxford, OX1 4AX
Tel: 01865 276920
Opening times: daily 9-5. Closed 25
December and Good Friday

ROUSHAM PARK
Nr Steeple Aston, OX6 3QX
Tel: 01869 347110
Opening times: daily 10-4.30 (last
admission); House April-September,
Wednesday, Sunday and Bank
Holidays 2-4.30 (last admission)

Shropshire

HAWKSTONE PARK
Weston, Shrewsbury, SY4 5LG
Tel: 01630 685242
Opening times: daily August 2-4.30

Somerset

HESTERCOMBE HOUSE
Cheddon Fitzpaine, Taunton,
TA2 8LQ
Tel: 01823 337222
Opening times: May-September,
Saturday and Sunday 2-5;
October-April, Monday to Friday 9-5

MONTACUTE HOUSE
Montacute, TA15 6XP
Tel: 01935 823289
Opening times: Wednesday to Monday
11.30-5.30 (or dusk if earlier)

TINTINHULL HOUSE
Tintinhull, Nr Yeovil, BA22 8PZ
Tel: 01935 822545
Opening times: April-October,
Wednesday to Sunday and Bank
Holidays 12-6

South Yorkshire

**WENTWORTH CASTLE
GARDENS**
Off Lowe Lane, Stainborough,
Barnsley, S75 3ET
Tel: 0226 772566 for opening times.

Staffordshire

ALTON TOWERS
Alton, ST10 4DB
Tel: 01538 702200
Opening times: daily mid-March-early
November 9-5

BIDDULPH GRANGE
Grange Road, Biddulph,
Stoke-on-Trent, ST8 7SD
Tel: 01782 517999
Opening times: April-October,
Wednesday to Friday 12-6,
Saturday, Sunday and Bank
Holidays 11-6; early November-mid-
December, Saturday and Sunday 12-4

Suffolk

HELMINGHAM HALL
Helmingham, Stowmarket, IP14 6EF
Tel: 01473 890363
Opening times: end April-mid-
September, Sunday 2-6

SOMERLEYTON HALL
Nr Lowestoft, NR32 5QQ
Tel: 01502 730224
Opening times: 12.30-5. April-June
and September, Sunday, Thursday
and Bank Holidays; July-August,
Tuesday to Thursday, Sunday and
Bank Holidays. House open 2-5.

Surrey

HAMPTON COURT
East Molesey, KT8 9AU
Tel: 0181 781 9500
Opening times: daily 7 to dusk

PAINSHILL PARK
Portsmouth Road, Cobham,
KT11 1JE
Tel: 01932 864674
Opening times: early April-mid-
October, Sunday 11-5. Group
visits on other days by
arrangement.

**ROYAL BOTANIC
GARDENS, KEW**
Richmond, TW9 3AE
Tel: 0181 940 1171
Opening times: daily from 9.30.
Closing times vary with the season,
call for information.

THE SAVILL GARDEN
Wick Lane, Englefield Green,
Egham, TW20 0UU
Tel: 01753 860222
Opening times: daily March-October,
10-6; November-February, 10-4

Warwickshire

PACKWOOD HOUSE
Lapworth, Solihull, B94 6AT
Tel: 01564 782024
Opening times: daily April-September
2-6; October 12.30-4.30

WARWICK CASTLE
Warwick, CV34 4QU
Tel: 01926 408000
Opening times: daily end October-end
March 10-6; every weekend during
August 10-7

West Midlands

**BIRMINGHAM BOTANICAL
GARDENS**
Westbourne Road, Edgbaston,
Birmingham, B15 3TR
Tel: 0121 4541860
Opening times: Monday to Saturday
9-8, Sunday 10-8 (or dusk if earlier)

West Sussex

BORDE HILL
Borde Hill Lane, Haywards Heath,
RH16 1XP
Tel: 01444 450326 or 412151 on
weekends
Opening times: daily mid-March-early
October 10-6

LEONARDSLEE GARDENS
Lower Beeding, Horsham,
RH13 6PP
Tel: 01403 891212
Opening times: daily April-October 10-6

NYMANS
Handcross, Haywards Heath,
RH17 6EB
Tel: 01444 400321
Opening times: March-October,
Wednesday to Sunday and Bank
Holidays 11-7 (or dusk if earlier).
Last admission 1hr before closing.

WEST DEAN GARDENS
West Dean, Chichester,
PO18 0QZ
Tel: 01243 811301
Opening times: daily 11-5
(last admission 4.30)

West Yorkshire

BRAMHAM PARK
Wetherby, LS23 6ND
Tel: 01937 844265 for
opening times.

Wiltshire

BOWOOD HOUSE
Bowood Estate, Calne, SN11 0LZ
Tel: 01249 812012
Opening times: daily April-October
11-6

THE COURTS
353 The Walk, Holt
Trowbridge, BA14 6RR
Tel: 01225 782340
Opening times: April-October,
Sunday to Friday 2-5

HEALE GARDENS
Middle Woodford, Salisbury,
SP4 6NT
Tel: 01722 782504
Opening times: daily 10-5

IFORD MANOR GARDENS
Iford Manor, Bradford-on-Avon,
BA15 2BA
Tel: 01225 863146
Opening times: April and October,
Sunday 2-5; May-September,
Tuesday to Thursday, Saturday and
Sunday 2-5. Other days and times by
appointment only.

STOURHEAD
Stourton
Warminster, BA12 6QD
Tel: 01747 841152
Opening times: daily 9 to dusk

Index